KU-511-069

FREEDOM THROUGH OBEDIENCE

The Ten Commandments
Explained and Applied

George M Philip

Christian Focus Publications

Dedicated
to
Joy, my wife and partner

All Scripture references are from the Revised Standard
Version of the Bible, unless otherwise indicated.

©1992 George M Philip

ISBN 0 906731 90 9

Published by
Christian Focus Publications Ltd
Geanies House, Fearn, Ross-shire,
IV20 1TW, Scotland, Great Britain.

Cover design
by
Seoris N. McGillivray.

Printed and bound in Great Britain by
Cox & Wyman Ltd, Reading

All rights reserved. No part of this publication may be
reproduced, stored in a retrieval system, or transmitted,
in any form or by any means, electronic, mechanical,
photocopying, recording or otherwise, without the prior
permission of Christian Focus Publications

Contents

THE TEN COMMANDMENTS
Exodus 20:1-17

And God spoke all these words, saying, I am the Lord your God, who brought you out of the land of Egypt, out of the house of bondage.

First: You shall have no other gods before me.

Second: You shall not make for yourself a graven image, or any likeness of anything that is in Heaven above, or that is in the earth beneath, or that is in the water under the earth; you shall not bow down to them or serve them; for I the Lord your God am a jealous God, visiting the iniquity of the fathers upon the children to the third and the fourth generation of those who hate me, but showing steadfast love to thousands of those who love me and keep my commandments.

Third: You shall not take the name of the Lord your God in vain; for the Lord will not hold him guiltless who takes his name in vain.

Fourth: Remember the sabbath day, to keep it holy. Six days you shall labour, and do all your work; but the seventh day is a sabbath to the Lord your God; in it you shall not do any work, you, or your son, or your daughter, your manservant, or your maidservant, or your cattle, or the sojourner who is within your gates; for in six days the Lord made Heaven and earth, the sea, and all that is in them, and rested the seventh day; therefore the Lord blessed the sabbath day and hallowed it.

Fifth: Honour your father and your mother, that your days may be long in the land which the Lord your God gives you.

Sixth: You shall not kill.

Seventh: You shall not commit adultery.

Eighth: You shall not steal.

Ninth: You shall not bear false witness against your neighbour.

Tenth: You shall not covet your neighbour's house; you shall not covet your neighbour's wife, or his manservant, or his maidservant, or his ox, or his ass, or anything that is your neighbour's.

*   *   *

INTRODUCTION

In the contemporary scene, theological, socio-
logical and psychological, there is an obsession
with man. Starting with himself, man is seeking to
find the solution to man, and it cannot be. We
must start with God. If we are not right with God,
and if we are not doing right by God, we will never
deal rightly with each other because by nature
man is self-centred. This is the doctrine of Scripture. Man is not a perfect creature but defective
and disordered. Every aspect of his personality
and all his varied capacities are marked, blighted
and vitiated by the fact that he is fallen from grace.
He needs to be set right with God and set right
within himself if he is ever to be set right with
others.

One of the tremendous needs in our generation is for the reintroduction of God: to the church
as well as to the world. He must be introduced as
the God who has spoken clearly and decisively;
the God and Father of our Lord and Saviour Jesus
Christ. This emphasis is necessary in view of the
vague talk about God as the "ground of being"
(Tillich), the "first cause" (Aristotle), a "principle

of righteousness". All these non-biblical terms tell us how man sees God. But what does that signify? Man is looking down on God, assessing and systematising Him in terms that man understands and is prepared to accept. God is being limited to the scope and capacity of human intellect and understanding.

Someone who had been an elder in the Church for years was deploring the non-churchgoing of the younger generation. He stated his own conviction to his minister, "I know there is something somewhere." That was the extent of his doctrine of God. If that is all a man can say, his religion is too vague to be any use.

If God is God, we must not indulge in the sin of setting up our private ideas of Him. Let the God who speaks, speak to us. Let the God who draws near, draw near to us. Let the God who makes Himself known, make Himself known to us. And let us be prepared to accept Him for what He is and for what He says He is.

"I am the Lord your God." There is a declaration that God is the God with whom we have to do. He stands alone and stands supreme. When God speaks, what He says is not up for discussion. We are too keen on discussion nowadays: it can be a great escape from the truth. What God says is certainly not open to qualification.

This then is why we study the Ten Commandments. They are God's words to us. We deal with them not as an exhaustive scholarly exercise in theology, but as a practical study in relation to living the Christian life.

Before we turn to them in detail it is useful to consider, from the Book of Exodus, the position of the Israelites at the time the Commandments were first given. There are three main points to notice.

First of all we should read Exodus 20:2:

> "I am the Lord your God who brought you out of the land of Egypt, out of the house of bondage."

This declares that salvation is by God's sovereign grace and power. He, and He alone, can save from bondage. This is something we need to engrave on our minds and hearts, because fallen human nature has a tremendous capacity for thinking of salvation in terms of self-effort and good works. Some people say, "You get to Heaven by keeping the Ten Commandments." In that case none of us will ever reach Heaven because none of us keep all the commandments. Salvation is not achieved by trying to keep the law of God, but comes by the sovereign grace and power of God. He *first* saved the children of Israel out of Egypt and *then* He gave them His law. Grace comes before law. All of God's law is set in the context of God's grace.

The second point to note is that the sin above all other sins amongst the children of Israel, as revealed in the first nineteen chapters of Exodus, is the sin of pride. Pride and "self" are expressed in a spirit of resentment. Time and again when God spoke to this people they resented it. Time and again, wherever and however God led His people, they resented His handling of their lives. This pride is still the curse of fallen human nature.

The third significant thing in these opening chapters is that they reveal the propensity for evil in a redeemed people. Think about it carefully. Israel had already done some terrible things and they were yet to do even more terrible things in defiance of God. And God knows full well the carnal or sinful capacity of fallen human nature. He is not taken by surprise. People sometimes say, "I never thought I would do that." But they do! Sometimes there stir within us thoughts, feelings, inclinations that disturb us deeply and we wonder why this should be. The story of the Book of Exodus reveals with devastating honesty the propensity for evil in fallen human nature. This highlights the need for God to speak His law.

Why were the Ten Commandments given? Paul answers that question in Galatians 3:19a, "It was added because of transgressions." That is, it was added to the human situation by God because of human sin, actual and potential. God's great design in giving the Ten Commandments was "that you may not sin" (Exodus 20:20).

The notion that they are there simply in order to condemn is false. God states clearly that He has given these ten good words of grace to keep us from sin. They are there to guard us in areas where we need to be guarded. He knows best where we are weak. What a respect and admiration we should have for God! What wonderful care and concern He has for us, because He knows full well what sin can do to us. He knows how easily we are tempted and enticed by the apparent attractiveness of sin, as the story of the Garden of Eden makes plain. If there had been no sin there would have been no need for God's law. But there is sin and so God gave the people His Ten Commandments.

We see why they had to be stated clearly and radically when we consider what people sometimes say about living by conscience. They may say, "I don't go to church, or read the Bible, or pray. I live by my conscience." We must not dismiss this out of hand. (Christians sometimes sweep people away far too readily. We are not likely to win them for Christ if we start by demolishing everything they say!) How do we deal with this business of living by conscience? Turn to Paul's Letter to the Romans 1:19, 20:

"What can be known about God is plain to them, because God has shown it to them. Ever since the creation of the world his invisible nature, namely, his eternal power and deity, has been clearly perceived in the things that have been made. So they are without excuse."

That is in complete harmony with people who say that they climb mighty mountain peaks in Scotland and, viewing the marvels of creation, feel a great sense of God. Before I was consciously a Christian I had the experience during the war of being on look-out at night on a big naval vessel and, as I became aware of the vastness of the skies and the power of the waves, I had a real sense of God. But when we read on through the passage in Romans we find that:

"Although they knew God, they did not honour him as God or give thanks to him" (Romans 1:21).

They were living by conscience: they had an awareness of God, but they were not bowing to God.

There is a verse in Scripture that speaks about the light that lightens every man that comes into the world (John 1:9 AV). Missionaries sometimes go to the strangest of places and realise that some people there are just waiting to be told about the God of salvation. I recall reading of how pioneer missionaries preached Christ to a people never reached before and one man said he always knew there must be someone like Christ. People have a sense of God and a sense of right and wrong.

"They show that what the law requires is written on their hearts, while their conscience also bears witness and their conflicting thoughts accuse or perhaps excuse them" (Romans 2:15).

However, when we have been "living by our conscience", there have been times when we have been aware that we were doing wrong and we have still done it. And conscience is not foolproof. Like every other faculty it is clouded and confused because, as the Bible clearly teaches, human nature is fallen. It is disordered. That is why we are such complicated creatures. But God, because He is a God of grace, was not prepared to leave us to live by our unreliable consciences. God spelled out how we should live, and He did it in a way that could be seen and heard and understood in absolute clarity.

The Commandments were not given at the beginning of the human story in the Garden of Eden, not even after sin had entered into the human situation, bringing all sorts of consequences and complications. Nor were they given at the new beginning after the Flood in the time of

Noah, though it was obvious, even then, that human nature had a tremendous capacity for evil and needed to be both curbed and directed. In these days the Bible says that:

> "The Lord saw that the wickedness of man was great in the earth, and that every imagination of the thoughts of his heart was only evil continually .... Now the earth was corrupt in God's sight, and the earth was filled with violence. And God saw the earth, and behold it was corrupt; for all flesh had corrupted their way upon the earth" (Genesis 6:5,11-12).

The Ten Commandments were still not given at the time of Abraham, when it was made plain that God's plan encompassed the whole course of human history.

> "The Lord said to Abram, 'Go from your country and your kindred and your father's house to the land that I will show you. And I will make of you a great nation, and I will bless you, and make your name great, so that you will be a blessing. I will bless those who bless you, and him who curses you I will curse; and by you all the families of the earth shall be blessed'" (Genesis 12:1-3).

We recognise, of course, that even in these early days God did speak to His people. For example at the beginning of Genesis 17, we find that the Lord appeared to Abraham and said, "I am God Almighty, walk before Me and be blameless." Down through the generations God both spoke and acted through Abraham, Isaac, Jacob and Joseph, and He has continued to do so right through the developing human situation which we call history.

Generations went past, and this passing of time was manifestly necessary, not least in proving to the children of Israel that apart from God they would never be anything but a total disaster. Their history right through the Old Testament demonstrates this. Every time the people turned away from God, sooner rather than later, they ended up in a mess.

This is one of the lessons we all need to learn, and it is sad that sometimes we are too proud to learn it: apart from God we will never be anything but a disaster. Such is the fallenness of human nature; such is the complication of our desiring and our thinking; such is the atmosphere and the pressure of the world; and such is the activity of the Devil. We cannot emphasise too often or too radically that apart from God we are bound to fail. It took all of the four hundred years to bring the Israelites to the point where they recognised that they needed God. They had not dealt with God realistically or personally for a long time. That may well be a basic lesson that some of us need to learn. It is so easy to forget God and close our ears to His Word. It is so easy to close our eyes and hearts to the lessons of the providence of God. It is so easy to stand back from every good and gracious influence that God brings to bear upon us.

It took four hundred years for God's purposes to ripen; four hundred years from the time of Abraham to the giving of the Ten Commandments. God judged that His people were then ready to be given His law.

In the New Testament (Romans 3:20) we read that no human being will be justified in God's sight by the works of the law since through the law comes the knowledge of sin. This highlights another great function of the Ten Commandments: to convict us of our sin and to persuade us that we are sinners. One of the most difficult tasks in a preacher's life is to persuade people that they are sinners. But when you consider the things we do, the things we say, the things we refuse to do; when you consider our reactions, and the basic self-centred ruthlessness in every single one of us, it seems strange that we find it so difficult to acknowledge that we are sinners. The Ten Commandments certainly help, because by the law the knowledge of sin comes home to the human heart.

Before we study the Commandments in detail

we must recognise that they fall into two sections. The first four have to do with our relation to and our dealings with God. Then come six which have to do with our dealings with each other. The order is basic: God first; man next. Nowadays we are plagued by everyone talking about man's rights, man's liberties, man's this, that and the other thing. Here, as elsewhere, the word "man" includes "woman" with no sexist overtones intended. We have to recognise that human nature, inspired and tempted by Satan, has always tried to put man first and to compel God to serve man.

Consider by way of illustration the story of the two thieves who were crucified at the same time as our Lord Jesus Christ. One of them, almost in the midst of his death's agonies, turned to Jesus and said, "If you really are the Son of God, save yourself and us." What he was saying was, "If God is real and the Gospel is real get us out of our predicament!" That is the cry that has been going on all the time, down through history: "Why does God allow this? Why doesn't God stop war? Why doesn't God abolish illness?" In a sense, people are shaking their fists at God and blaming Him for everything, especially those things that spoil our enjoyment of life. That is putting man first.

But the Bible teaches us that God comes first. Turn to the story in Genesis 3:1-7. The Serpent is best spoken of as the "Shining One". The Devil can make sin appear very attractive. He is good at his job. He suggested to the woman that a God who denies you what is natural is a strange God. He went on to cast doubt on the idea of a God who punishes, suggesting, as he still does, that this is a rigid and extreme theological position. The Devil denied the serious consequences of sin, saying, "You shall not die." The woman took the forbidden fruit, involved her husband in the wrong, and at once discovered that taking what God had forbidden led to disaster, not to life and fulfilment.

The lie of the Devil was that by refusing God's way humanity would reach the peak of achievement and be like God. It is still the same today. History proves this as mankind blunders from crisis to crisis.

But some say, "What about all man's magnificent achievements, not least in the realm of scientific discovery?" Yes, man has triumphs, but along with all the achievements for good there are equal achievements of potential for evil. In the realm of literature people have achieved much. But while on the one hand we have writing that touches the deepest springs of human hope and aspirations, alongside we find bookshops crowded with shelf upon shelf of books which are rotten and corrupting. Man, even at his best, is a victim not just of circumstances, nor of the system, but of his own personality.

Turn to Romans 7:15, 18b-21:

"I do not understand my own actions. For I do not do what I want, but I do the very thing I hate .... I can will what is right, but I cannot do it. For I do not do the good I want, but the evil I do not want is what I do. Now if I do what I do not want, it is no longer I that do it, but sin which dwells within me. So I find it to be a law that when I want to do right, evil lies close at hand."

What a predicament! What inability! What incapacity! Theologians call this the state of total depravity. That does not mean that everybody is as bad as they could be, because there are restraints of training, fear, circumstances and self-interest. A Salvation Army officer, speaking to young people, once said, "Sometimes you have the temptation to sin but you do not have the opportunity. At other times you have the opportunity but not the temptation. But God help you if you have the temptation and the opportunity at the same time. There is simply no saying what you might do and what you might eventually become".

Total depravity does not mean we are as bad as we could be, but it does mean that if we are to be saved from sin, reconciled to God and changed so that we can live to please God, then God Himself

must do it. Have we not all at times found ourselves saying from the very depths of our being, "I
wish I were different!" The moment we admit
that, the God of the Ten Commandments, the
God who gave His Son Jesus Christ, says, "I can
change you."

That takes us back to the beginning of our
passage in Exodus 20:1,2:

> "And God spoke all these words saying, 'I am the
> Lord your God, who brought you out of the land
> of Egypt, out of the house of bondage."

Between Israel and all that was past lay the Red
Sea. There was, by the gracious act of God, a
complete break between what they had been in
the past and what God had made them now.
Sometimes when we are trying to urge upon people the need to be saved so that they will go to
Heaven and not to Hell, we emphasise that between Heaven and Hell a great gulf is fixed.
Likewise, for those who stand in God's salvation,
between their past and present there is a great
gulf fixed. Every now and again people appear out
of our past and say that they remember us. But
theologically they are wrong. In Christ we are
different persons. We have not simply turned
over a new leaf or adopted a new lifestyle; we are
different, totally, in identity and nature.

> "If anyone is in Christ, he is a new creation: the old has passed away; behold, the new has come" (2 Corinthians 5:17).

So, for the children of Israel, as they stood and trembled at Mount Sinai, God's saving act stood between them and the past. Their sins were forgiven. They were delivered from bondage. A new life was theirs. How had that life to be lived to please God and to do His will? How were they to find fulness of life and peace and joy? God spoke, and gave His people Ten Commandments, ten good words of grace.

The Ten Commandments and the New Testament

Sometimes when people are challenged about their attitude to the Ten Commandments they dismiss them as being irrelevant because they claim that they no longer apply to "New Testament Christians". Jesus Christ did not teach that.

Look at part of what He said in the Sermon on the Mount:

> "Think not that I have come to abolish the law and the prophets; I have come not to abolish them but to fulfil them. For truly, I say to you, till heaven and earth pass away, not an iota, not a dot, will pass from the law until all is accomplished. Whoever then relaxes one of the least of

these commandments and teaches men so, shall be called least in the kingdom of heaven; but he who does them and teaches them shall be called great in the kingdom of heaven. For I tell you, unless your righteousness exceeds that of the scribes and Pharisees, you will never enter the kingdom of heaven" (Matthew 5:17-20).

Christ made it clear that God's law must not be swept aside. Indeed He set the standard higher, in the words, "You have heard... but I say to you," (Matthew 5:21ff). He insisted that the principle of the law had to do with the heart and life and not just with outward conformity to the letter of the statute-book.

The Ten Commandments still apply, and not only in terms of outward observance, for the Pharisees did that. Jesus tells us that our righteousness must exceed theirs if we would enter the kingdom of Heaven. There is no question of "relaxing" the Commandments and teaching others to do the same. There are serious consequences in doing so, just as there are "benefits" in keeping and teaching the Commandments. No matter our claim to be a Christian, if we say and do not act, if the law of God and our daily life are two separate compartments, if our church life does not determine our life in the world, we are Pharisees and Jesus says we will not enter the kingdom.

There is of course a difference between how the Pharisees and Jesus regarded the law, as Matthew 23 makes clear:

> "Then said Jesus to the crowds and to his disciples, 'The scribes and the Pharisees sit on Moses' seat; so practise and observe whatever they tell you, but not what they do; for they preach but do not practise. They bind heavy burdens, hard to bear, and lay them on men's shoulders ....
>
> Woe to you, scribes and Pharisees, hypocrites! For you tithe mint and dill and cummin and have neglected the weightier matters of the law, justice and mercy and faith; these you ought to have done without neglecting the others. You blind guides, straining out a gnat and swallowing a camel!" (Matthew 23:1-4; 23,24)

Over the centuries the Pharisees added many extra regulations to the law of God and these man-made restrictions and requirements came to be the focus of their attention. They approached Jesus in Matthew 15:1, not to ask about His teaching or His miracles but to ask, "Why do your disciples transgress the tradition of the elders? For they do not wash their hands [a ritual washing] when they eat." To which Jesus replied, "And why do you transgress the commandment of God for the sake of your tradition?"

The difference between the Pharisees' emphasis on petty details of legalism and the Lord's emphasis on the spirit of the law is most obvious in their attitude to the Sabbath. The Pharisees condemned the disciples for plucking a few ears of corn on that day because they were hungry (Matthew 12). This was considered to be harvesting! Jesus defended the disciples, not because the Sabbath was unimportant but by referring them to the Scriptures:

> "If you had known what this means, 'I desire mercy, and not sacrifice,' you would not have condemned the guiltless. For the Son of man is lord of the sabbath" (Matthew 12:7,8).

The point at issue with the Pharisees was not the validity of the Fourth Commandment but how it was to be understood. Christ showed that it was a day for doing what pleases God; the Pharisees saw it as a day for keeping hundreds of meticulous rules, added and insisted on by the traditions of their forefathers.

When Christ healed on the Sabbath this difference burst into prominence. Compare the different attitudes in Luke 6:6-10 and 13:10-17. Jesus looked with compassion on the man with the withered hand and the woman who had been ill for eighteen years; the ruler of the synagogue was indignant and the Pharisees were filled with fury. Jesus here exposed the hypocrisy of the situation just as he did in John 7:19 when He challenged the antagonistic Jews by saying, "Did not Moses give you the law? Yet none of you keeps the law. Why do you seek to kill me?" After all, plotting murder breaks the law more significantly than plucking ears of corn.

Some may doubt the continued relevance of the Commandments because Jesus did not spell them out in the Gospels. Of course He was addressing Jews who had been taught the law of God from infancy. At times He specifically referred people to the Commandments (Luke 10:25,26; Matthew 19:16-22). He also summed up the essence of the law in terms of loving God with the whole heart and loving our neighbour as ourself (Matthew 22:36-40). This is very different from a legalistic attitude of keeping rules about the Sabbath and about religious behaviour. The problem in our day, of course, is not concentration on the letter of the law but disregard of it altogether.

At this point some may demur and refer to the fact that Paul says that we are "not under law" (Romans 6:14). But that has to be taken in context. Paul is speaking of the basis of salvation and there is no suggestion whatsoever that we can earn salvation by keeping the Commandments. The law convicts but only Christ can save. The law fulfils its function when it leads us to the Saviour (Galatians 3:24 A.V.). It is by faith in Christ and the inward working of the Holy Spirit that the just requirement of the law is fulfilled in us (Romans 8:4). When we stray from God's way the Commandments speak sternly to us to turn us back to Christ in whom alone is found salvation and life.

The importance that Jesus placed on keeping God's commandments is seen in how He spoke of them on His last evening with His disciples:

"If you love me, you will keep my commandment" (John 14:15).

"He who has my commandments and keeps them, he it is who loves me" (John 14:21).

"If a man loves me, he will keep my word" (John 14:23).

"He who does not love me does not keep my words; and the word which you hear is not mine but the Father's who sent me" (John 14:24).

"If you keep my commandments, you will abide in my love, just as I have kept my Father's commandments and abide in his love" (John 15:10).

What better can we do than study the commandments given to us by God?

THE
FIRST COMMANDMENT
No Other Gods

When God spoke in Exodus 20:2, giving His people the Ten Commandments, He identified Himself:

> "I am the Lord your God who brought you out of the land of Egypt, out of the house of bondage."

He declared Himself, not as the God of creation, although He is that; nor did He speak as the God of providence who rules over all things, although He is that as well. He spoke as the God of redemption. He was saying to the people, "I brought you out of the land of Egypt. Nobody else heard your cry; nobody else took any notice of you; nobody else came to help you; nobody else could set you free; nobody else had plans for you; nobody else set value upon you; but I did." What a God! And on that basis He declared and insisted, "You shall have no other gods before Me".

"You are mine," says God, "and I don't go in for sharing."

In the story of the Book of Exodus the stage had been reached when Israel had to go forward to the service for which they had been saved. God is not like some foolish "do-it-yourself" characters who make things and then wonder what to do with them. He had a clear and glorious objective when He saved these people, just as He had clear objectives for us when He saved us. If we say we cannot see the beginning, let alone the fulfilment, of God's purposes it is because we are having to wait: not because God is slow, nor because He is incompetent, but because we are not ready.

Time is part of God's process. This is a lesson that is hard for us to grasp because we live in an "instant" generation. We go in for crash courses to learn quickly. Few want to spend years in training. Many Christians want to learn a few techniques and then launch into service. We want quick results, on all sorts of levels, including that of evangelism. That is not the way God works. But Christians are, in many ways, infected by the spirit of the age. We want everything now. Some of the older generation have told me how, after years of saving, they bought their first carpet and were delighted with the achievement. Now, most people want fitted carpets in every room and all the gadgets right from the start! We have lost the sense of achievement. No one wants to wait for anything.

Even if, for various reasons, we choose to wait, there comes a time when *we* decide *we* have waited long enough and God should act. Take for illustration the rather delicate subject of starting a family. It is so easy to take control and when we decide it is suitable, we expect God, the giver of life, to act instantly. If He does not do so we feel hard done by. We feel deprived because we are not being given the fulfilment we desire. I speak of these human situations with utmost sympathy but, just as I take myself to task when I preach, I must speak the truth to you. Our lives need to be in God's hands, to be administered by Him. The great danger is that we take over the administration, we take charge, and we make the decisions; and it is at this point that God says, "You shall have no other gods before Me."

In Exodus the Israelites were about to go forward to the service for which they had been saved. What had they to do? First of all they had to be God's people. That is the beginning of all service. God always wants us before our service. They were called to be God's people, and as such to do His will. To do that they needed more than the liberty God had given them when He took them out of the slavery they had known in Egypt. Liberty is a great thing, but can it be handled rightly? I once wanted to be free, but I made such a mess of things that freedom from God is the last thing

I want now. Instead I love the hymn that says, "Make me a captive, Lord, and then I shall be free." The people needed more than liberty, because being free from adverse circumstances and from oppression can only be an unmixed blessing if human nature is perfect and integrated. But human nature is not like that.

Therefore, if these people were going to be a real "people", and not just a crowd (there is a big difference), a people with identity, stability and usefulness, then they needed to be shown how to be right with God and how to be right with each other. The only person who could say what was needed was God, and God spoke and gave them the Ten Commandments.

Does "You shall have no other gods before me," simply mean "God first"? That is a good and necessary lesson to learn. In every aspect of human life, relationships, and activities, God must come first. Some time ago a Christian man said to me, "It is really quite simple once you get your priorities set." It was great to hear that. Lots of things are very simple once you recognise what takes priority. You do not have to agonise for guidance; it is there. "You shall have no other gods before Me."

Is "God first" all that the commandment means? There is more. We must realise something of the greatness of the God who knows His people and speaks to His people in a personal way. He blesses His people without waiting for their deserving. This is the God over against whom, or with whom, there is no equal. Go back in the story to Exodus 15:11-13, 17,18, the Song of Moses:

"Who is like thee, O Lord, among the gods? Who is like thee, majestic in holiness, terrible in glorious deeds, doing wonders? Thou didst stretch out thy right hand, the earth swallowed them.

"Thou hast led in thy steadfast love the people whom thou hast redeemed, thou hast guided them by thy strength to thy holy abode.

"Thou wilt bring them in, and plant them on thy own mountain, the place, O Lord, which thou hast made for thy abode, the sanctuary, O Lord, which thy hands have established.

"The Lord will reign for ever and ever."

There is no other like God. Think of how the prophet Isaiah spoke of God:

"He will feed his flock like a shepherd, he will gather the lambs in his arms, he will carry them in his bosom, and gently lead those that are with young.

"Who has measured the waters in the hollow of his hand, and marked off the heavens with a span, enclosed the dust of the earth in a measure and weighed the mountains in scales, and the hills in a balance?

"Who has directed the Spirit of the Lord, or as his counsellor has instructed him? Whom did he consult for his enlightenment? .....

"To whom then will you liken God, or what likeness compare with him?

"Have you not known? Have you not heard? Has it not been told you from the beginning? Have you not understood from the foundations of the earth? It is he who sits above the circle of the earth, and its inhabitants are like grasshoppers; who stretches out the heavens like a curtain, and spreads them like a tent to dwell in.

"To whom then will you compare me, that I should be like him? says the Holy One. Lift up your eyes on high and see: who created these? He who brings out their host by number, calling them all by name; by the greatness of his might, and because he is strong in power, not one is missing.

"Have you not known? Have you not heard? The Lord is the everlasting God, the Creator of the ends of the earth..."

(Isaiah 40:11-14, 18, 21-22, 25-26, 28).

God says to His people, "If once you see who I am and what I am; what I say and what I have done; what I am doing and what I will yet do; then you will see the folly of ever turning away to any other god. I am God; there is none else. You shall have no other gods before Me."

But Israel lived in what we now call a pluralist society. There were territorial gods and there were nature gods. Many regarded the sun, or the moon, or the stars, or the wind, or the storm as gods. There were gods of fear. There were gods that required human sacrifice. Israel lived in a generation, and in an area of the world, where people believed that there were gods at war among themselves. Many people were never quite sure if their god was stronger than the god of a neighbouring nation and they lived in a state of dread.

Think of that marvellous story in 1 Samuel 5 about Dagon and his temple. When the Philistines captured the Ark of God and put it in their temple, the idol Dagon was toppled off its perch. What a tragedy for people who regarded Dagon as their great god! They rallied round and lifted Dagon back on to his pedestal. Next day he was down again. It must have been terrible to discover that the god you trusted in was no use. Some people, nowadays, say they trust in luck. It is sad when you find even Christians at times saying, "Touch wood." What kind of wood? An idol? Another god? A "something somewhere" that you trust in, but not the God of the Bible? "You shall have no other gods before Me."

In the pluralist society of the time there were many gods that stirred up and let loose human passions: gods that could cause men and women to give themselves in blind frenzy to death. Compare that with some twentieth century activities and interests that make people uncontrolled and uncontrollable. One Saturday afternoon I switched on the radio and when I heard the chanting, the calls, the whistling and the roaring at a football match, I was glad I was not there. There is an idolatry in sport that makes some people uncontrollable. The authorities are increasingly worried and they do not know what to do. Appeals to people to control themselves have no effect.

A similar thing is seen in an idolatry of politics. I worry about politicians, not about statesmen, but the latter are in very short supply! Sometimes, listening to the words of politicians I recall what the present generation never knew: the throbbing power of Hitler's speeches in Nazi Germany in the late 1930's. A strident voice, repeating, repeating, repeating, caused hundreds of thousands of people to cast aside every consideration and restraint. They committed themselves to follow Hitler's lead with blind frenzy. Think of what we have read more recently in the newspapers about certain fanatical Muslims who were prepared to load up a car with high explosives, drive it to its target and blow themselves up with it. I, for one, still recall the time when the Royal Navy ship I was on was heading towards the Japanese war area. All of us knew full well that there were "kamikaze" pilots who were prepared to point their planes right at us. The fact that they would die was quite irrelevant. The Emperor required it! That is the idolatry of false gods.

Think of the god of the "state". We see it clearly when we look back to Hitler's Germany, Stalin's Russia, Idi Amin's Uganda, and many other forms of totalitarian states, including the now-discredited Marxist form of the state. Never believe that the Marxists are interested in individual working people. The Marxist philosophy essentially despises the working class, regarding it simply as a tool to be made use of to bring about what they would call the ideal state. But when the state becomes god, it is not very long before we end up with George Orwell's "Big Brother".

There is idolatry in sport, in politics and in pleasure. Through and through society there is an idolatry of gratification. It is quite frightening. There is a verse in the New Testament that speaks of people who are lovers of pleasure rather than lovers of God (2 Timothy 3:4). To get their full measure of pleasure they will sacrifice anything, even their families. Joy Davidman, in her commentary on the Ten Commandments, entitled *Smoke on the Mountain*, speaks about men's gods and what these gods do to them. She speaks about the god of sex, held out as the ultimate fulfilment of life: away with moral standards; away with those outdated institutions of marriage; go for what you want. The result is disillusionment and disintegration.

She goes on to speak of the god of science, and many people do make it their god. They believe that science can explain and solve everything, even though many scientists say at once, "Oh no, we can't." But there is an idolatry of progress: the scientific advance which will get everything under control; it is the ground of all hope; there is no need in this enlightened day to go back to all the ancient out-of-date stuff about God. Of course, we do not underestimate the achievements of science, but along with all the good achievements there have come massive complications.

We could go on extending the list Joy Davidman gives of false gods. There is the false god of career. How many broken families there are, up and down the country, because the man, or the woman, of that family has dedicated himself or herself to a career, and everything, including the welfare of children, has had to give way. There is the god of popularity. Many, including ministers of the gospel, bow at this shrine. There is the great god of social convention. People can be unhappy about certain activities but they go on with them because it is expected. Who expects it? God? No: other people.

False gods are powerful. This is one reason why we need the ballot box. We have proved over the past two decades at least that the old practice of deciding things by a show of hands is no longer any use because the false gods, be they the state or the Trade Union, are so powerful that grown men with great experience find themselves just not able to put up their hands and vote publicly against the false gods. We need to thank God that still in our country we have the ballot box.

Recognise, as Paul teaches in Corinthians, that behind many things and many movements there is a motivating spirit that is evil: the Devil! God says, "Don't go that way. Don't go to other gods, because they will destroy you. Look to Me, trust Me and listen to Me." We must not listen to contemporary philosophers who speak of God as "the ground of being." What a ghastly phrase! You cannot pray to "the ground of being." When your heart is broken because your nearest and dearest is at death's door, you cannot go for comfort to "the ground of being." Nor must we speak of God as the "first cause" or the "under-lying principle of nature" or the "principle of righteousness". Speak of God as the God who made Himself known in the Garden of Eden, the God who came looking for His lost man, the God with a sob in His voice saying, "Adam, where are you? You had Me, what else could you possibly need?"

The First Commandment says, "Let God be God." There are too many people who pronounce about Him and say, "Oh, I don't think God would do that!" Have they a comprehensive knowledge of God? They seem to think so! Too many people ask why God doesn't do this; why God doesn't stop that; why God allows hurricanes and earthquakes. One answer is that when God created the world it was very good. It was man who brought nature down and disordered it. It was man who caused it to be so frightening. (Genesis 3:17-19; Romans 5:12; 8:19-22.)

Listen rather to the voice that says, "Be still and know that I am God. You shall have no other gods before Me. Bow down before Me, listen to Me, rest in Me and trust Me. Don't give way to your fears and uncertainties and appetites. Don't go back into that kind of bondage." Think carefully of what Paul says in Romans 8:35-39.

"Who shall separate us from the love of Christ? Shall tribulation, or distress, or persecution, or famine, or nakedness, or peril, or sword? ...... For I am sure that neither death, nor life, nor angels,

nor principalities, nor things present, nor things
to come, nor powers, nor height, nor depth, nor
anything else in all creation..."

These are the kind of things people are afraid
of; things to which people bow down; things which
dominate people. They press in on us all the time,
but none of these things has the power to separate
us from the love of God which is in Christ Jesus
our Lord. God is greater than all!

In Deuteronomy 6:4 the Commandments are
urged on the people with the words, "The Lord
our God is one Lord." That verse should make us
think of God as the God of peace, in whom there
is no disharmony, no uncertainty of purpose, power
or issue. He is the Sovereign God. He is the God
who brought His people out of bondage.

He is the God who gave His Son for us. Do you
know any other god who has done that? He spared
not even His own Son but gave Him up for you and
for me. That Son of God, who came and lived and
died, is the One who said, "I came that they may
have life, and have it abundantly" (John 10:10).
Jesus Christ is the One of whom the Scriptures
declare that there is no other name under Heaven
given among men by which we must be saved
(Acts 4:12). God says, "Look unto me, and be ye
saved, all the ends of the earth" (Isaiah 45:22
A.V.). When you look, what do you see? In the

midst of the throne of God you see a Lamb, as it had been slain (Revelation 5:6 A.V.). Through all the endless ages of eternity, at the heart of the glory of God, we shall see the price of our salvation. Then, far more than is ever possible now, we shall honour the name that is above every name.

Please God you and I will be among the ransomed of the Lord who see Him face to face, who bow the knee and cast our crowns before Him.

"I am the Lord your God who brought you out of the land of Egypt. You shall have no other god before Me." God is saying, "Have Me as your God." What an offer!

THE
SECOND COMMANDMENT
No Images

It is a basic premise of the Christian faith that God speaks to people, and in so doing makes plain what they are to believe concerning Himself and what duty He requires of them. The Ten Commandments were given so that His people should know clearly what He is like and what He requires. They are given to inspire and to enable us to be the kind of people that God wants us to be: to keep us from doing things and from going in directions that would harm and even destroy us. They are God's good words, full of grace, and pointing the way of life.

Remember that the Ten Commandments are introduced by a statement from God concerning His person and His saving activity. He stands supreme and answerable to no one. He is sovereign in every sense. We may not like such a God and, away back in Exodus 5, Pharaoh, the king of Egypt, certainly disliked Him, demanding contemptuously, "Who is the Lord that I should obey His voice? I do not acknowledge Him and will not obey Him." But whether we like God or not, whether we accept Him as He is or not, whether we believe in Him or not, has no effect whatsoever on the fact that God is.

This brings us to the Second Commandment. If we are to worship God and walk with Him, we must do so on the basis of God as He really is, and not as we think He is.

"You shall not make for yourself a graven image."

All our representations of God are bound to be defective. We cannot compare Him to anybody or anything within our experience, and therefore any attempt we make to picture God is necessarily flawed. In pastoral visitation a minister some-times meets people who say, "I think of God this way," or "I like to think of God as being ..." or "I don't think God would do that." But such ideas are irrelevant. Someone who had been receiving our church magazine for years but had never been in Sandyford once decided to pay a visit. She said to me, "Mr Philip, you are not a bit like what I imagined." I had to say, "I am sorry about that, but this is what I am." You see the danger. If we just imagine what God is like, we will probably be wrong.

Images and representations of any kind are not

only defective, they are dangerous. They can misrepresent God and we become preoccupied with our idea of God rather than seeking to learn from the Bible about God as He really is. The images are not necessarily ugly things; they can be lovely and very artistic, but they tend to deceive and to take us away from God. But God wants us for Himself. He is a jealous God and claims His people in love. He is not prepared to share us with another. Would a happily-married person share their partner with anybody? Of course not. In the right sense we are jealous. And so is God. He says, "I have redeemed you and paid the price to set you free. I have named you with My name, and I have loved you with My love. You are My people." I am glad that God is jealous, if it means that He wants me and refuses to share me. He is in earnest, as Exodus 20:4-6 shows.

At Mount Sinai, where the Ten Commandments were given, the people heard God but they saw no form (Deuteronomy 4:12). That is very important because it emphasises that, in the whole of our life as the people of God, it is God's Word to which we must listen. Moses emphasised that they heard God speaking, but there were no visions or apparitions, no signs of angels, nothing that they could see and retain in their memories to remind them of their experience. It is God's Word that we too must live by, not our ideas of God, nor our experiences of God, and certainly not our private revelations of God. We are dealing with the objective reality of God, who reveals Himself and speaks to us in a way that we can understand.

If we begin to depart from God's Word, what God has said concerning Himself, we end up with the idea of a God who is simply the projection of our own thoughts. This causes confusion. Some who are quite happy to discuss the theory of religion say that people with a sense of insecurity or ambition have projected this into the idea of a God. Others suggest that the idea of God is just the residual legacy of primeval fears and inhibitions, and we have "invented" God as a prop to make us feel all right.

Men are always trying to dispose of God, but we are dealing with objective reality, not fiction or imagination. Whatever the limitation of language, the Christian speaks of God "up there". The Bible speaks of God separate from, and above, His creation. He knows what is going on. He is not only up there, He is out there, and down here. Never think of God as being tremendously remote. In the giving of the Commandments we see the God who came right down to His people to speak to them. If we refuse to listen, we are left to live on our own with our fears, phobias, limitations, complications, uncertainties and our total lack of capacity to cope.

The Second Commandment tells us to let God be what He says He is and forbids the making of any image or likeness, whether material, or pictorial, or in the mind. If we do end up worshipping God as we think He is, rather than as God says He is, what we will really be doing is using our idea of God to allow us to do what we want. That is one real danger of making images.

When we have distorted ideas about God we land in all sorts of difficulties. We can think of Him as just waiting for us to sin so that He can smite us in judgment. That is not the God of the Bible. If we think of Him as one who holds back His goodness from us because we have not properly and fully confessed our sins, then we end up with a God of fear, and that is the kind of god the pagans have. Those who worship idols are never sure whether their god is pleased with them or not, nor at all sure what he will do to them. That leads to a life of terror.

Others are sentimental about God. Some people say, "I like to think of Jesus playing with the children." There is nothing wrong with that; He spoke about children's games. But that is only one selective aspect of what God is like. Some people seem to think of Him as a kind old grandfather. Perhaps they recall their own grandfather with some lovely memories and within minutes they have forgotten about God as He really is, thinking of Him in terms of a particular human being. If they mean a grandfather in the benevolent sense, then God is indeed kind and gracious to His children and to His children's children; but He is so much more than just a kindly man.

Some people tend to think of God in terms of "superman". But we all have different ideas as to what superman is, or looks like, or should be. We must not make a fictional character of our superman but, if we think of God as someone all-powerful, someone mighty to save; if we are thinking of Him whose name is Jesus, who in the middle of the storm on the Sea of Galilee rebuked the wind and waves and caused them to be calm, then we have caught sight of God as He really is. But human ideas of God are limited. We can end up making God in our own image, and that is deficient and dangerous. In Isaiah 55:8,9 God says, "My thoughts are not your thoughts .... For as the heavens are higher than the earth, so are my ways higher than your ways and my thoughts than your thoughts." In the Second Commandment God says, "Deal with Me as I am; I have shown you what I am."

We have not been speaking of images in an ugly or coarse sense, but there are ones like that. Some who have been in distant parts of the world will have seen images of repulsive and grotesque figures, in homes and shops, and sometimes lining the roads leading up to magnificent temples. There can be a fascination about these figures, and tourists get out their cameras, but we must remember that there are people whose thinking about God is conditioned by and expressed in these distorted carvings and pictures. Some of the "images" are of hard-faced gods; some many-headed, many-handed; some representing the goddess of fertility; some representing the false god we find in the stories of the Old Testament, the Fire God, Moloch, who required his devotees to sacrifice their babies so that he might be propitiated and might perhaps be prepared to look favourably upon them, or at least not to be too angry with them.

The people who made these images were in measure expressing their ideas of God. Not many of us would carve images like that, but are there, perhaps, other things we worship? In *Smoke on the Mountain*, Joy Davidman begins her chapter on images in this way:

"What shape is an idol? I worship Ganesa, brother, God of worldly wisdom, patron of shopkeepers. He is in the shape of a little fat man with an elephant's head; he is made of soapstone and has two small rubies for eyes. What shape do you worship?

"I worship a Rolls-Royce model, brother. All my days I give it offerings of oil and polish. Hours of my time are devoted to its ritual; and it gives me luck in all my undertakings; and it establishes me among my fellow men as a success in life. What model is your car, brother?

"I worship my house beautiful, sister. Long and loving meditation have I spent on it; the chairs contrast with the rug, the curtains harmonise with the woodwork; all of it is perfect and holy. The ashtrays are in exactly the right place, and should some blasphemer drop ashes on the floor, I nearly die of shock. I live only for the service of my house, and it rewards me with the envy of my sisters, who must rise up and call me blessed. Lest my children profane the holiness of my house with dirt and noise, I drive them out of doors. What shape is your idol, sister? Is it your house, or your clothes, or perhaps even your worthwhile cultural club?"

These are things that people live for. These are the things for which people can always make time, things to which people are prepared to devote meticulous care and energy. These are the things that, without their noticing, become their god. As God has said, "You shall have no other gods before Me. You shall not make for yourself a graven image."

The matter of idols leads us on to the question of superstition. I shall never forget driving up through Thailand in an air-conditioned, very comfortable bus, complete with television set, and draped over the driver's mirror were "spirit garlands". These garlands of fresh flowers were renewed each day as they were supposed to keep away the evil spirits and give a safe journey.

We may see the danger in spirit shrines and garlands paid for by frightened poor people, and say that is the road to bondage. We may see the danger in bowing to idols of wood and stone, but how do we regard the superstitions in this country, superstitions held by many who would be very angry if you called them pagans? Yet one will have a rabbit's foot in his pocket, beautifully done, sometimes with a silver or gold band, very expensive, and many more have "good luck" bracelets.

What of those who are fascinated by magic, the supernatural and the occult? These are strange and dangerous areas of experimentation whose inspiration may be "spirit" but it is not the good Spirit of God. And what of those who consult fortune-tellers or read horoscopes? Are not all these transferring their trust away from the real God to a god who is imaginary? This is why God says, "You shall not make for yourself a graven image or likeness of any thing that is in Heaven above, that is in the earth beneath or that is in the water under the earth."

Leaving false worship, we turn to apply the

commandment to Christian practice, where we must consider the whole range of visual aids and dramatic representations which can in fact stop our thinking short of reality and can hide God. Take this as an example: coming back from a conference, several ministers were discussing a lecture on Children's Addresses. Reference was made to a young man who was "absolutely at the top" in that field. His friend outlined one magnificent illustration which went on and on. Someone eventually said, "What was the lesson?" There was total silence. Nobody spoke. The teller of the story said, apologetically, "I've forgotten." He remembered the illustration in detail, but he forgot the message. That is a warning to all who like to use visual aids. Be very careful. The audience may remember you, and the illustration, but not God.

Perhaps a little more seriously, and without being sectarian in the wrong sense, I think of those who regard a crucifix as an aid to devotion. The truth of the matter is that such an image or representation is defective because it focuses on the physical sufferings of Christ and forgets the facts of victory and of glory. The Christ who once died on the Cross is no longer on the Cross. He was crucified, dead, and buried; He descended into Hell. The third day He rose again from the dead, ascended into Heaven and sits on the right hand of God the Father Almighty. If we are still thinking of a Christ nailed to a Cross then we have stopped short.

Take a different kind of illustration. Think of many children's books where Jesus is pictured as a man with a rather weak face. An impression of feebleness is not true to Him who is the strong Son of God. Think of Christmas cards. So many of them have an emphasis on the sentimental. You seldom find one that shows the stable with the shadow of the Cross already falling over it. But Christ who was born in Bethlehem was born in order that He might die.

Another reason why there must be no image or likeness of God is that it has the effect of externalising religion. It puts religion "out there" instead of "in the heart", making it something outside ourselves, something at a distance, something that we handle without it being a part of ourselves. This setting up of a likeness, a very close representation of God, enables us to retain ourselves for ourselves. Religion becomes something mechanical, a routine or an action which *we* have invested with significance. But, for example, we do not need to "light a candle" to indicate our care and prayer for another, nor do we pray to a lifeless statue. We can go to God through Christ, and speak to Him directly. He is a God who wants to listen and who answers prayer.

Sometimes a building or a minister can get in the way of God. The Jews of Jesus' day thought more of their temple than of God. Some people, if they cannot be in their own church on a Sunday ,say, "It's not the same." Others tell their minister, meaning it as a compliment, "When you are not there, I just don't seem to be able to get through to God." If that is so, the sooner God takes away the minister the better! He has become a hindrance.

Even the Sacraments, Baptism and the Lord's Supper, instituted by our Lord as true and valid symbols, can be a distraction. People make the symbol an end in itself. They say, "I was baptised here." That is not the point! Have you come in faith, through Jesus Christ, to yield your life to God? There is danger even when we come to the Lord's Table. I am not necessarily speaking of those who tend to venerate the bread and the wine as if they were the very body and blood of Christ being broken and poured out all over again. I am thinking rather of those who say, "I have been to Communion." What does that mean or do for you if you have not come to the Christ who is represented in Communion?

Making images or likenesses of God has the effect of externalising religion and worship. It has also the effect of materialising God, making God less than spiritual. What does that mean? In the business of religion, evangelical and otherwise, too many people indulge in the creating of an atmosphere. If you want to reach this group or that group you must create the right atmosphere. This is essentially manipulation on a fleshly level, trying to inculcate a "feeling" of God. Some people when they get down on their knees to pray spend half their time trying to produce within themselves a feeling of God by way of preparation for prayer. If the "mood" does not come they "feel" they cannot pray. This is not faith! You can end up with all sorts of feelings which may or may not be of God. They may well be from the evil spirit of the world which is Satan, not God.

God is, whether we have a feeling of Him or not. When we pray, God hears our prayers whether we feel it or not. We live by faith, not feelings. It is dangerous trying to awaken a feeling of response. Too many preachers indulge in this kind of thing, and do it quite deliberately. But that is not the same as awakening the response of faith. Feelings without some mental understanding of the truth preached are of no real value. Some people, if a service has made them feel all weepy or excitable, conclude that it must have been good; but a surge of feeling is not the same as spiritual worship. "God is spirit, and those who worship him must worship in spirit and truth" (John 4:24), engaging all the highest and varied capacities of personality.

This is what makes true worship such a therapeutic thing. It engages not the lowest, the physical, the sensuous capacity, but all the highest capacity of mind and will and spirit.

There is another section of Scripture relevant to our theme which is disturbing and devastating. It is Romans 1:22-25. It teaches that in images or representations of God, whether physical, mental or emotional, there is a progressive, degenerative tendency. Men do not like to retain God in their thinking so they build up their own selected representations of Him. This displaces God, which in turn makes man God, which in turn begins to unman man and sets in motion the process of degeneration of life and personality which brings us to the kind of carnal brokenness and debasement of society as we now know it.

Of course, in its more refined forms, this displacing of God with images and representations leads to pride: the pride of superiority compared to others. People do not go so far as to say, "I have a better God at home than you have." But there is a tendency to idolise (and we use the word deliberately) our own spiritual experience.

Some, and this needs to be said plainly, are quite unteachable because they "speak in tongues". Some are quite unteachable because they are under the impression that they have a private telephone line to God and they are sure that they get all their direction unmistakably and personally from Him. Some are unteachable because at some time or another they saw a vision. Do you know this passage in Job 4:12-16:

"Now a word was brought to me stealthily, my ear received the whisper of it. Amid thoughts from visions of the night, when deep sleep falls on men, dread came upon me, and trembling, which made all my bones shake. A spirit glided past my face; the hair of my flesh stood up. It stood still, but I could not discern its appearance. A form was before my eyes; there was silence, then I heard a voice."

That has a "ghostly" sound. And the speaker was belabouring Job, one of the mightiest saints of God. This critic, on the basis of some experience which made his nerves tingle and the hair at the back of his neck almost stand on end, felt sure he must be spiritual. From the point of this experience onward he considered himself to be an authority on spiritual things. But the experience that he had was not of God, because its effect was to make him proud.

Images are dangerous, and even likenesses or representations of God are limited. They can serve as blinds rather than windows. They are limited because they are created by us. They are distorted because they are selective. They are dangerous because they tend to promote ritual and observance rather than communication with God, fellowship with God and instruction from God. God says, "Do not set up any image or likeness that would distort and conceal Me. I come to you as I am in the multitude of my mercy, and in the eternity of my love. Have Me."

When God speaks to me like that I find my heart strangely disturbed that ever I should have been tempted to look anywhere else but into the face of Him who loved me and gave Himself for me.

THE
THIRD COMMANDMENT
God's Holy Name

The Third Commandment is a declaration backed up by a warning: "You shall not take the name of the Lord your God in vain; for the Lord will not hold him guiltless who takes his name in vain."

Whatever is the exact significance of the commandment, one thing is clear: God takes the matter very seriously.

An example of breaking this commandment was seen some time ago in an article by the literary critic of a prominent Scottish newspaper. The writer, who had a fine command of English, was reviewing a book in a penetrating way. By way of illustration and emphasis she gave a list of well-known names in the literary world; she paused with a comma, added the words, "and good God," and then completed the list. These three words seemed quite fortuitous. They were not necessary to make the point and they simply revealed that the writer was, in the strict sense of the word, profane. She evidenced no sense of reverence for the name of God nor for all that the name signified. She had no thought of the sensitivities of those whose faith in God is real and reverent. The name of the Lord was taken in vain.

Very often nowadays, in radio and television programmes of the interview type, whether the interviews be of comedians, sportsmen or politicians; in programmes of entertainment, whether "soap-operas" or detective stories; and even in the kind of programmes that tend to be watched by children, references to "Good God", or "My God", are slipped in with no justification whatsoever. We are living in a generation in which this casual use of the name of God has increased significantly, so that it is accepted by many as commonplace. There are some people for whom I had considerable respect in the past but now I refuse to listen to them because I have heard and watched them on television trotting out the name of God as if He were the least valuable thing in the whole of creation.

It should disturb us deeply, because the abiding commandments of God say, "You shall not take the name of the Lord your God in vain." There is a passage in the Letter to the Hebrews which speaks about "trampling underfoot the blood of the Son of God". That is exactly what they are doing.

The habit of devaluing His name signifies that the God of the Christian Gospel is far from the thoughts of those using it. If they thought of Him in even a remotely Biblical sense, they would not speak with such casual indifference. The Bible explains the attitude of the unbeliever: "God is not in all his thoughts" (Psalm 10:4 AV), and "There is no fear of God before his eyes" (Psalm 36:1 AV). He does not really believe that God is God. He does not reckon on God's involvement in life, nor that He is entitled to take him to task. But Proverbs 29:18 (AV) says, "Where there is no vision, the people perish." Where there is no reverence for the name of God there is no reverence for the person of God. And when there is no reverence for the person of God, the next step is the degradation of "God" which Paul speaks about in the first chapter of Romans. This leads to human deterioration and then self-destruction, and it brings society under the rebuke and judgment of God.

It could help at this point to consider the sequence of the first three commandments. They are about things we must not do, and it is necessary that they should be negative, because God is aware of the potential we have for going wrong. What would the result be if we were left to ourselves with no restrictions? Would we rise up to be paragons of humanity? I think not. We know how easily we go wrong and how perversely we choose wrong. This is why God speaks negatively: "You shall have no other gods before Me": a commandment that speaks about the supremacy, the uniqueness and the sovereignty of God; let God be God. "You shall not make for yourself a graven image or likeness of any kind": let God be who He says He is; keep clearly in mind that *none* of our ideas about God have validity unless they conform to Scripture revelation.

When we come to the Third Commandment, think how the whole of human history testifies to man's tendency to dislike authority, and to debase and spoil what is good and pure and true. Think of what man has done, for example, to the concept of love. Man has made it a tawdry thing that has more to do with animal desire and emotional lust than with love. It is exactly the same with the name of God. We have an inbred tendency to debase the name of God. The way people use His name makes it plain that they do not believe in Him. They do not take Him seriously. They are deposing Him, taking Him down from His throne and making Him a nothing. Not only are they deposing God when they use His name irreverently, they are trying to dispose of Him.

The Third Commandment brings us into the realm of all that we mean by profanity and blasphemy. For our safety we are warned, "You shall not take the name of the Lord your God in vain; for the Lord will not hold him guiltless who takes

His name in vain."

Behind this commandment and its prohibitions there lies the principle that a name is not empty. A name expresses a person, and people who use a name identify with and unite themselves with that person. One of the best illustrations of this is a football crowd. You hear them shouting, for example, the two syllable chant, "Rangers, Rangers!" or "Celtic, Celtic!" Watch the crowd. They are not standing casually. It is not a crowd of separate individuals. They have become one unified whole. They are not chanting the name as an empty thing. They are willing their team to do certain things. They are identifying with the team, not just associating with it. They are seeking to exercise a power over the team. As the crowd wills on the team, the team is joined with it, and they with the team, and the effect of this is seen in the wanton destruction all over the city after the occasion of "worship." It is not football any more; it is idolatry. The name has called into being powers and passions, and has let them loose in a way that is very frightening.

The same kind of thing operates, for example, in the using of the name of Satan. Some years ago I was watching a play on television that had to do with a boys' school. The evil character was one of the boys and the whole situation was being engineered into Satanism. It was being presented as entertainment; or was it? What was the motive behind the thinking of the writer of the play? Towards the climax there was an altar, and round it a group of schoolboys, led by the bad one were repeating, "Satan, Sa-tan, Sa-tan." They were *using* the name to invoke the person; and in so invoking the person they were seeking to identify with the person, and to cause him to operate in their interest and to fulfil their purpose. Consider carefully Isaiah 8:19; Leviticus 20:6; 1 Corinthians 10:19-20 and recognise that tampering is dangerous. People should never trifle with anything Satanic.

There are parties where "for fun" the name of Satan is spoken. They say it is not serious; there is no thought of committing themselves to darkness and evil. People dabble in the use of evil names and can think it harmless, until they find themselves involved and trapped. Be very careful of that kind of thing, especially if it involves repetition of names or formulae or incantations, even if they seem religious. If you ever find yourself near that kind of thing, run for your life. Have nothing to do with it because there is power in a name. Names are not empty.

This is a very serious matter for a generation of unbelief. By and large most people have stopped believing in God or the Devil in any real sense. They no longer reckon on the power of God and the power of the Devil as actual elements in human experience. As a whole, most do not believe in the reality of the world of angels, spirits and the Devil, nor do they believe in our involvement with that spiritual world and our association with it. Nor are we aware, as we should be, of how much the powers of the world to come impinge upon us. It is in this context that we affirm that a name is not an empty thing. The name is part of the person and is used not only to gain access to the person but power to use the person.

There is the same principle with regard to the using of the name of God. You must not use the name of the Lord in vain because there is power in that name. Turn to some New Testament illustrations: first of all in Acts 3:16, the story of the healing of the lame man at the gate of the Temple. Peter affirmed that it was by the name of Jesus, by faith in His name, that the man was made whole. The miracle, done in the presence of the crowd, was by the name of Jesus. There was no "performance" or "build-up", no emotional repetition of the name "Jesus, Jesus," trying to create the atmosphere that would produce a result. It was all matter of fact. "Silver and gold have I none, but what I have I give you. In the name of Jesus Christ, rise up and walk." Peter lifted him up on his feet and the man was healed. The deed was done by the name of Jesus. But it was not just the name, it was the Jesus represented by the name.

Consider now Acts 19:13-17, the fascinating story about the renegade priests, the sons of Sceva. It is a picture of men "using the name" of Jesus. It is laughable but serious. They were religious charlatans trying to "cut in" on a popular movement that had extraordinary manifestations. They really said, "In the name of Jesus whom Paul preaches, we command you." The evil spirit replied, "Who do you think you are?" They used the name, but they had no right to the name, because they did not belong to Jesus. They got the fright of their lives. Do you see what they were doing? They wanted to make use of the name of Jesus for their own ends. If they could use the name of Jesus to cast out demons and to heal people, they were "made". Think of the plans, the power and the popularity! Think of the fees! But they were using the name of the Lord in vain.

It still happens. There are many causes, some good and some bad, which want to use the church, or God, to support their particular interests. When they speak in that way they are using the name of the Lord in vain because they do not have faith, nor do they commit themselves to the Gospel of the name of Jesus.

Some commentators point out that this commandment has particular application to taking oaths, and making promises or vows. A minister, for example, uses the word "vow" at a wedding. "In the presence of God and before the face of this congregation will you now make your vows one to the other?" That is, in the name of God, will you make your vows? Can such vows ever be broken without guilt in the presence of God?

We have the same emphasis when admitting new members to the church by public profession of faith, "In the presence of God and before the face of this congregation you are now required to make your vows and to answer the appointed questions," that is, to make promises in the presence of God. We are calling upon God to witness, to seal and to ratify what is being done. We are calling upon the name of the Lord. But if we do not mean what we are saying, and if we do not hold to what we have said, then we have taken the Lord's name in vain. Recall the words of Ecclesiastes 5:5:

"It is better that you should not vow than that you should vow and not pay."

The time comes when the Lord sends His messenger to ask for the fulfilment of the vow. If we say we did not really mean it, then we took the name of the Lord in vain. At times I think back to the vows that I took before God and before the congregation at my ordination; I gave my answers in the presence of God, calling upon His name.

The Third Commandment also applies to religious speech. We have the petition at the beginning of the Lord's Prayer, "Hallowed be Thy Name." But in practice do we who call ourselves Christians really "hallow", value as holy, the name of the Lord? Sometimes we speak of the Lord God Almighty in a way that is far too "casual" and familiar, in a way we certainly would not speak to our employers, or to our school teacher. It is not a good sign when the name of the Lord is always tripping off people's lips thoughtlessly in incidental conversation. There is an irreverence which moves quickly into the realm of blasphemy.

The commandment applies even further to the realm of religious speech. Jesus said, "Why do you call me 'Lord, Lord,' and not do what I tell you?" (Luke 6:46). Our words say, "Lord, Lord," but our lives say quite differently. We do what we choose, not what God commands. Speaking pious words while living self-centred lives is in fact to take the Lord's name in vain.

This leads on to the question of false profession: involvement in Christian activity without the corresponding heart-commitment and obedience of life. Think of the words of our Lord Jesus Christ in Matthew 7:22-23:

> "On that day many will say to me, 'Lord, Lord, did we not prophesy in your name, and cast out

demons in your name, and do many mighty works in your name?' And then I will declare to them, 'I never knew you; depart from me, you evildoers."

Their lives proved that they did not belong to Him. People can be involved in Christian activity and have a spiritual reputation and yet they do not in any real sense belong to the Lord.

Taking the Lord's name is not a casual or an innocent thing, because the name is not empty. People say, "What's in a name?" The Bible says a great deal is in a name. The name of God signifies the person of God and the power of God. We read in scripture, "Whoever calls on the name of the Lord shall be saved" (Joel 2:32; Acts 2:21). Now, calling upon the name of the Lord is not a magical formula; it is an appeal, and a commitment, to the God of the name and His saving power in Jesus Christ. To call upon the name identifies you with the person and with the power of the person. That is why the name must always be handled carefully, because we cannot use the name without being drawn close to the reality behind it.

Even where it is recognised that the name is associated with the power of the person named, there is danger in using it. It is all too easy to reach the stage of using the name to try to get the power, or the person, or God to do what we want. Think, for example, of people in prayer-meetings asking God for some extravagant things, adding in passionate repetition, "We ask it in the name of Jesus." People "claim" things in the "name" of Jesus without seeking God's will in the matter; without being sure that it is what the Lord wants. This is not spiritual but psychological, and it is dangerous.

"The name" is a phrase often used in a very arbitrary and high-handed way in the realm of faith-healing, and for a great many people it degenerates into a simple process of giving orders to God. I heard of a man in this kind of situation who said to his friends, "Oh, but God must heal. I claimed it in the name." But God did not heal and the person did die of cancer. Something was claimed. But this was not the action of faith. It was rather presumption because it went beyond the measure of faith (Rom. 12:3), and whatever is not of faith is sin (Rom. 14:23). If it is not in the will of God then it is not in the name of God, for the will and the name are both "in" God.

Think of the story of Elijah and the priests of Baal in 1 Kings 18:17-39. The priests of Baal called upon the name of their god, but there was no result. Elijah called upon the name of the Lord. What a contrast there was! The servants of Baal spoke and acted with intensity and frenzied repetition. Both words and actions were pressurised.

By contrast, Elijah was calm and quiet and prayed in faith on the basis of what he knew of God and God's will. Elijah called upon the name of his God and God answered with power. Elijah's God is real.

Our generation has virtually stopped believing in a God who does things. Psychiatrists say patronisingly, "We all need our god," suggesting that the concept of "god" is something in our imagination to which we appeal, not a God who acts. The scientists speak about life-force and laws and principles, but not about a God who does things. But God is real. He is not to be trifled with. Nor is His name to be trifled with. There is power in the name of Jesus. The name has been given to men, and "there is no other name under Heaven given among men by which we must be saved" (Acts 4:12).

You may say that the commandment refers to "the Lord your God", and we are talking about Jesus. What did Jesus say in John 17:6? "I have manifested Thy name." What did He mean? He had shown people what God is really like. He had made God plain. What is God like? What is the name of God to mean to us? God commended His love toward us in that while we were yet sinners Christ died for us. He is the God who calls all men everywhere to repent and to believe. He is the God who has given Jesus a name that is above every name, that at the name of Jesus every knee shall bow.

There is an old Redemption Hymn that says, "Take the name of Jesus with you," not as a lucky charm, but in the sense that you take the Jesus of the name, the Son of God who loved you and died for you, who lifts you up and keeps you safe and brings you to God in everlasting salvation. Take the name of Jesus with you, and treasure it, because there is no other name under Heaven, given among men, by which we must be saved.

How do we react to those who do take the name of the Lord in vain? Do we just ignore it, as an accepted thing in society? Do we simply feel hurt or angry? Should we not pray for them and for the opportunity to speak about this serious matter? Are we prepared, at the right time, to challenge those who speak lightly the name of God and of His Son Jesus Christ, and to do it graciously without insulting them, so that they may see that the name has meaning, and may set a guard over their hearts and mouths?

You shall not take the name of the Lord your God in vain: for the Lord will not hold him guiltless who takes His name in vain.

THE
FOURTH COMMANDMENT
God's Holy Day

This commandment, which is stated in more words than any of the others, begins with a statement, clear and concise, "Remember the sabbath day to keep it holy."

It emphasises that we must keep holy something which God has already made holy. We are called to *keep* the Sabbath. It is God who has *instituted* it. The commandment goes on to be quite specific in relation to our own keeping of the Sabbath and to our responsibility to enable and to encourage others to keep it. The emphasis is on enabling rather than on imposing. The final statement of this commandment declares the Sabbath to be grounded in God's activity, pattern and example in Creation.

In studying the first three commandments we have become aware that we are dealing with prohibitions that are comprehensive and absolute but not merely negative. They are commands of God's grace, and their objective is *not* to deny man all the things that he wants to do. People say,

"If you take the commandments too seriously, what kind of life would you have?" The answer is, "If you don't keep the commandments, what kind of life do you have?" It will be the sordid kind of life we read about in our daily papers. The objective of the commandments is not to narrow down and limit man's experience and fulfilment; nor is it to prevent man's self-expression in a safe way. But there is self-expression that is manifestly dangerous; there are aspects of human personality that the Lord God must prevent us expressing for our own good, and for the good of society. The Ten Commandments are designed and set forth to keep mankind safe and to preserve us all from the inevitable degeneration that comes when human nature is left to itself.

If human personality, life and society are to hold together, God says, "You shall have no other gods before Me. You shall not make any images of Me. You shall not take the name of the Lord your God in vain, *and* you shall remember the Sabbath Day, to keep it holy."

The Fourth Commandment carries the same authority as the first three, and it also carries the same authority as the later ones with regard to killing, and the other moral wrongs and horrors that scar the face of mankind. We may not deal seriously with the first three and then with the last six and sit lightly to the fourth. It is not for nothing that the commandment concerning God's Sabbath is found right at the very heart of the law.

Remember that these commandments were given by the God of salvation. "I am the Lord who brought you out of the land of Egypt" - that is how Exodus 20 begins. God speaks in this way so that He might make it plain that salvation *has been* accomplished. It does not depend on keeping the Ten Commandments. God said then and God says now, "I have saved you, irrespective of your deserving and independent of your help. You could neither do it yourself nor contribute to it. In terms of salvation you are an empty-handed beggar." That is why so many people do not like the Gospel: they do not like to think of themselves as empty-handed beggars. But in respect of salvation that is exactly what we are: we have nothing to give, there is nothing we can do, nothing we can contribute. God has given salvation to us. But the potential for degeneration is still there in our human nature and personality.

Paul speaks in Romans 7:14-18 as a believing man and expresses in vivid terms the inescapable and ongoing battle with sin. He finds it to be a law or a principle that when he wants to do right, evil is there to resist him. A hymn-writer expresses this truth with profound accuracy when he says:

"And they who fain would serve Thee best
Are conscious most of wrong within." (Twells)

It is no exaggeration to say that history testifies to man's capacity for getting things wrong. It is part of fallen human nature that man always tries to do whatever he is doing without God. We need the Sabbath to be reminded of God, to be made aware of God, to turn back to God, and to take time to meet with Him and to listen to His words.

In the beginning of the story of human history, in the Garden of Eden (Genesis 3), we find the account of how man was persuaded to believe that the way of life was to be found in ignoring God's commandments. When we move into Genesis 4 we have the story of Cain and Abel: tension, resentment, confusion and murder; possibly the first example in history of the perennial conflict between the "haves" and the "have-nots", between those who felt they were accepted and had "made it", and those who felt they were not accepted and were rejected. But Cain was in the position of not having and not being accepted because he chose it to be so. He declined to live by the commands of God and he ended up in bitterness against both man and God. When we come to Genesis 6 the human situation had so degenerated that it is recorded that God regretted that He had made man. He did not regret that He had made the world. He made it "and behold *it* was very good."

Whatever we mean by the six days of Creation

(and we are not to be side-tracked by that issue), God in His appointed time made the whole order of creation. In six days the work was completed and on the seventh day God rested. He rested, not because He was tired but because His work was perfectly done. The first "seventh day" was a day to rest in, to rejoice in, and to draw all the benefits and pleasure from a work completed. Right from the beginning of human history God appointed this pattern for the men and women in His world: six days were days for working and the seventh day was a hallowed day, a day for resting, in all the full significance of what it means to rest.

Resting is not necessarily the same as doing nothing. You can spend a whole day doing nothing and at the end be more tired than if you had been at work. But there is a totally different kind of rest which refreshes and revitalises. The Sabbath is different from the other days. We may protest that we do not see the difference. That is irrelevant. Without spectacles some people cannot see things properly but the things are still there. Whether or not we can see how one day can be different from other days, the fact remains that God has declared that He has made one day different from all other days, and it has to be kept different, because that day was the token, the sign and the seal of a finished work.

In Exodus 20, when the people of God were at

a significant point in their development with regard to the future, we find God speaking to them through Moses the law-giver: "Remember the Sabbath Day, to keep it holy." In other words, do not do anything that will make unholy this day that God has sanctified. For illustration, think of it this way: children are aware of what happens if Mother has washed the kitchen floor and then they come in from playing football and walk on the newly- washed floor with muddy boots. They are spoiling something that has been made clean. In this commandment God says, "Don't put any dirty marks on my holy day."

In the Book of Exodus the Sabbath Day is spoken of as far back as chapter 16. In the story of the giving of the manna, the heavenly food was provided for the needs of the people. They were commanded to gather it day by day and on the sixth day to gather two days' supply. They were not to gather on the Sabbath Day. But some stupid and stubborn people would not listen to Moses. In self-confidence they went out to gather as usual. They found nothing! It is strange that people who have received so much from God can at times sit so lightly to God's holy commandments. There is an example of this in Isaiah. The people of God were distorting the observance of the Sabbath Day. Up to a point they gave lip-service to God, but that is no substitute for heart-obedience.

If you go to church on Sunday morning and spend the rest of the Lord's Day, or Sabbath, doing things that displease God and fail to do what pleases Him, it gives people, especially neighbours, the impression that Christians are hypocrites, and that the Ten Commandments have been revoked. But be clear that a traditional observance of the Sabbath that has more to do with what people expect than with what God calls for, is *not* keeping the Sabbath holy.

God takes the Sabbath seriously. And it is not just a matter of conforming to a religious pattern. In Isaiah 58 the people ask God:

"Why have we fasted, and thou seest it not? Why have we humbled ourselves, and thou takest no knowledge of it?" (3a).

And God replies:

"Behold, in the day of your fast you seek your own pleasure, and oppress all your workers. Behold, you fast only to quarrel and to fight, and to hit with wicked fist. Fasting like yours this day will not make your voice to be heard on high" (3b, 4).

He goes on to say:

"Is not this the fast that I choose: to loose the

76

bonds of wickedness, to undo the thongs of the yoke, to let the oppressed go free, and to break every yoke? Is it not to share your bread with the hungry, and bring the homeless poor into your house; when you see the naked, to cover him, and not to hide yourself from your own flesh? (6,7).

"If you turn back your foot from the sabbath, from doing your pleasure on my holy day, and call the sabbath a delight, and the holy day of the Lord honourable; if you honour it, not going your own ways, or seeking your own pleasure, or talking idly; then you shall take delight in the Lord, and I will make you ride upon the heights of the earth; I will feed you with the heritage of Jacob your father, for the mouth of the Lord has spoken" (13,14).

Contrast this with the attitude of many religious people who regard Sunday as an irrelevance. We read in newspapers of local citizens and visitors alike reviling Scotland, complaining, "What is there to do on a Sunday?" Many think it a fair criticism. But is it not a tremendous reflection on human nature and what it has become that, if any occasion arises in which activities and entertainments are not available, it has, by its own confession, become incapable of either interest or pleasure? Is man as pathetic as all that? Do we believe that we need to be surrounded constantly, seven days a week, with all sorts of artificial stimuli just to keep us happily occupied? That is a denial of human dignity.

As each week comes round the great command goes out from the throne of God to stop, so that people, ceasing from their feeble, frightened scurrying around, might be enabled to hear the word of God's grace. That word is not only a declaration of salvation but a word that both awakens and satisfies the hunger for destiny in the hearts of men and women. In a very real sense the heart of this commandment is a call to refuse to submit to being mere creatures of senses and circumstances.

I remember a story told in my youth in the North East of Scotland concerning "The Laird of Udny's fool." I was tremendously impressed as a young boy hearing how that limited man, seemingly far below-average intelligence, said on one occasion, "Dinna bury me like a beast." It was sad that society had so devalued simple people that he had to ask that. But the world we have created for ourselves persists in its attitude that the Word of God should be eliminated, and this is a process that increasingly reduces us from the dignity of our humanity to the level of the beast, the mere creature. That is one reason why so much human behaviour now is the behaviour of the animal rather than of man made in the image of God.

One corrective to this dehumanising tendency is to "Remember the Sabbath Day to keep it holy."

We need to make it our business to preserve the Sabbath. Perhaps we should all be writing to our Members of Parliament with regard to any legislation in parliament concerning Sunday trading. At one point there was only one of the main chain stores in Inverness which did not trade on a Sunday, and Inverness is known as the capital of the Highlands. Traditions about the Sabbath do not prevent this kind of thing. It needs conviction about the authority of the Word of God and commitment to Christ, regardless of the cost. Do we refuse to shop on a Sunday? Are we prepared to write in defence of the Sabbath? Remember that a whole flood of individual letters is far more effective than organised petitions.

The keeping of the Sabbath is a command of God, and because it is a command it has to be kept. It is to be kept not just because the Sabbath is beneficial, although it is; it is to be kept not just because breaking the Sabbath hurts others and causes them to be involved in what they should not be involved in on the Lord's Day; it is to be kept because God instituted this seventh day principle as a basic element in the order of creation. It is built into God's plan for the working of the world.

If we have a car or any other piece of machinery, we read the instruction book. If the manual underlines that on no account must this, that, or the other be done, we will make it our business to remember the warning, because the maker's instructions tell us that if we ignore it we will spoil the machine. Now the great Maker of the universe gave instructions as to how His creation would work as He had planned it should, for our good and for our blessing. One instruction is, "Remember the Sabbath Day, to keep it holy."

Some try to dodge the issue by quibbling about which day is meant: Saturday, the Jewish Sabbath, or Sunday, Christ's Resurrection Day. As early as the year AD 100 the Lord's Day had taken the place of the Jewish Sabbath in the context of Christian worship. The arguments about this are well known but the important thing is to keep one day in seven. Whatever we call it, we remember both the day when creation was completed and God rested, and the day in which salvation was completed, the Resurrection Day when Christ's grave was left empty.

There is, however, a wrong way to keep God's holy day. By the time our Lord Jesus Christ lived upon the earth the Sabbath had become a terrible tyranny. The commentators tell us that in those days the Pharisees had a list of 1,522 things that people were not allowed to do on the Sabbath. These Pharisees, who insisted on the importance of over one and a half thousand rules centring on negative issues, were the very people who plotted murder and took the Son of God and nailed Him to the Cross. To this day there are those who are too much concerned with rules and with *not* doing things because of what the neighbours will think, rather than in doing things and in not doing things because God looks upon the heart. That is legalism and it is negative. It is not keeping the Sabbath holy.

People can go too far the other way and say, "It is the spirit of the law that matters, not the letter of the law." True, but only on Jesus' terms. In the Sermon on the Mount Jesus said, "You have heard it said... but I say unto you..." He sets the standard higher not lower! Take Jesus' words with regard to adultery: "Thou hast heard it said, 'Thou shalt not commit adultery.' " That is the letter of the law and it stands. But what of the spirit of the law? Jesus said that if a man looks on a woman and lusts in his heart, he is guilty. It is indeed the spirit of the law and not just the letter of the law that is important.

When we discuss this matter of the Sabbath, people tend to talk about their reaction to childhood Sundays and I grant that in past days, and no doubt in present days, there has been a fair amount of inhumanity whenever religion has degenerated into form and custom. But personally, Sunday has memories for me that are precious and this was in the context of a non-churchgoing family; the children were sent to church but the parents did not go. And yet, by the very nature of Sunday, when so little was allowed by way of activity, that day became a family day. For a variety of reasons one of the joys of Sunday to me was simply this, that Sunday could not be like the other six days. What a lifting of the heart of a young boy that was. It was different. It was a family day. I was sorry one Sunday evening when I asked permission to go to a secular concert in the village hall. I will never forget how my heart sank when the responsibility for decision was passed to me. My mother said, "You can go if you want." I went, and felt guilty.

My memories of Sunday are not memories of tyranny, and please God, the memories of my own children concerning Sunday will not be memories of tyranny even though it is difficult for a minister to be fully a father on a Sunday when he is so occupied with the necessary work of God's house. Such was the impact made upon me by my childhood Sundays that when I was in the Royal Navy it still influenced me for good. I was not a Christian in these days. No-one had told me how to find God. I had been in Sunday School since I was three, and in the Boys Brigade and Bible Class until I was eighteen and entered the Forces, and nobody had told me how to find God. I had never heard the word "converted". What a tragedy! Yet, in the Royal Navy, in the Naval Base of Scapa Flow, in the depth of winter, I would round up a few fellows from the North East of Scotland that I knew by name, to get them to change into Sunday uniform and go with me from the cruiser anchorage to the NAAFI canteen for the Presbyterian service. I was not a Christian, but Sunday was Sunday and I knew it, and I went to church.

The Sabbath principle, this one day in seven, was built into the order of creation, and right from the beginning of human history in the Garden of Eden, in regular sequence, one day was set apart to remind man of God, to enable man to rejoice in God, and to find fulfilment of life as God planned it. This holy day that was sanctified and ordained for the whole of human history was given to man so that man could be God-loving, God-satisfying and God-satisfied. But man's sin entered in and caused confusion in the whole situation. All the more reason then to remember the Sabbath Day to keep it holy.

If we forget to do so it will soon have an effect. For example, people in hospital find that every day has the same routine. Sometimes when we visit they will ask, "What day is it?" They are confused. Things do not seem right. When all days are the same we lose our bearings. I can remember during the last war when on duty at action stations there was scarcely any time to sleep. We tended to lose track of the days and then, when things went quiet afterwards, it took a considerable time before we got the pattern of our lives sorted out again. In the same way, if you lose the Sabbath Day you soon lose the place. If you lose the place you lose God.

During the French Revolution those who wanted unquestioned authority tried to abolish Sunday. They knew their job. Get rid of Sunday and you will soon get rid of religion. By and large our generation has got rid of half of Sunday. That is why so few churches have any activities after lunchtime on that day. We have got rid of half of the Lord's Day and our churches are half-empty. If we get rid of the whole of Sunday it will not be long before most of our churches are completely empty. But it is interesting that very soon the leaders of the French Revolution had to bring back Sunday for health reasons. The nation began to crumble under a system of life that demanded seven days of work.

Some people may say there is no need for this emphasis on one particular day as, living in the Gospel era, every day is holy. Every day may be holy but, human nature being what it is, every day very soon becomes ordinary. In Heaven all God's plans will be complete and death and struggle will be no more; in this world man's experience is still a struggle, but every seventh day God says, "Now stop. I will tell you something. There is a day coming when all struggle will be over. There is a day coming when your life will no more be wracked by temptation, fears and doubts. There is a day coming when all that I have promised will be yours." God says, "Until then, remember the Sabbath Day to keep it holy."

In the quiet of God's holy day, we must learn to do what God did on the Sabbath. We must rest. We need to take time to think of the God who made, the God who saves, the God who has called us to His eternal glory. It will not be long till the Lord's eternal Sabbath is here and then His servants shall serve Him and they shall see His face. Until that day comes, guard your Sundays. Remember the Sabbath, to keep it for God. Do not dare disturb and bring disorder into the pattern of life that God, the giver and satisfier of life, ordained from the beginning of time, for all people, believers and unbelievers alike.

THE
FIFTH COMMANDMENT
Honour to Parents

The commandment, "Honour your father and your mother that your days may be long in the land which the Lord your God gives you" (Exodus 20:12), is repeated and amplified in Deuteronomy 5:16, "Honour your father and your mother, as the Lord your God commanded you, so that" (first of all) "your days may be prolonged and" (secondly) "that it may go well with you, in the land which the Lord your God gives you." The two statements of the commandment must be held together.

Having stated the Fifth Commandment it would be easy to jump to conclusions and to assume that young people are the target. But there is nothing to suggest that the Ten Commandments, and this one in particular, were addressed primarily to children. Indeed they were spoken and applied to adults and parents. Their example, influence, pattern and disposition of life would be copied by the children. This is something we need to learn in both human and spiritual terms. We may teach our children the most excellent lessons of biblical and spiritual truths and do so with the tongues of men and of angels; but it is much more likely that our children will copy our way of life rather than conform to our verbal teaching. Therefore it is essential for adults who bear influence of any kind, especially those who are parents, or who may yet become parents, to take the commandments seriously. If they enshrine God's laws for healthy living in the world He has made and which He rules, then we are not studying something that belongs to the distant past but something that has immediate and practical application to our own day and generation.

The first four commandments have been concerned with our relationship with God. Now we are concerned with social involvement, and the prime responsibility here begins in the home. This commandment has at its heart a tremendous emphasis on the importance of the family unit, family loyalty, family discipline and family continuity. And the truths and principles which apply on the human level apply also on the spiritual level. When we speak about the domestic family we speak also of the church family, and therefore this commandment has a wide and penetrating application.

If we apply the commandment first on the social level it concerns the whole issue of the well-being of the nation. The result of keeping it is: "That it may go well with you in the land which the Lord your God gives you." When this commandment is forgotten the consequences are serious. Society can be strong, healthy and happy only when the marriage bond, and with it family life, are held in highest honour. This shows the seriousness of the modern attack on family life, and the moral and emotional rottenness of society is a solemn commentary on the trend. Read Romans 1:30 and 2 Timothy 3:2 where you find ghastly lists of the hideous sins of corrupt society. At the heart of both the lists you will find "disobedience to parents". This indicates that breaking the Fifth Commandment is of far-reaching significance. It means that a society which is marked by "disobedience to parents" is one that has gone dangerously far along the road of godlessness.

We begin then to see that the concept of family, in its structure and in its loyalty, is something that God has set right at the heart of human well-being.

Since this is so, we pose the questions: Are we properly aware of what is happening to society in our own day? Are we aware of how much we are contributing to what is happening to society? Is it not the case that for many, family life is disintegrating? This is not a case of glorifying the "good old days", which were often grim and deprived, as those who lived through them can testify. The old days were far from perfect! But older people speak with real nostalgia of family gatherings, of young people meeting together in each other's homes, and of times of speaking and singing together in a caring and healthful atmosphere. Family life was real, family bonds were strong and lasted as the children grew, married and set up their own homes. But this has largely disappeared.

There are many reasons: one of them is the gleaming little screen that is in the corner of most homes nowadays. It dominates so many lives. It used to be the case when the minister went into a house, especially if it was to arrange the details for a funeral service, that cigarettes were put out and television sets were switched off. But in a home recently the volume of the television programme was not even turned down, even for the arranging of the funeral of the father of the family. Something has gone very far wrong with family life and family values.

We must ask more penetratingly why it is that family life is ceasing to be the kind of thing that it once was, and as it is portrayed in Scripture. Is it because parents cannot be bothered with young people gathering in the house, disturbing the peaceful routine and making the place untidy? Is it because children are obsessed with what they call their "freedom" and would rather be anywhere than in their own home? Is it because either parents or children or both are demanding privacy and independence, or is it because parents and children alike are desiring secrecy? As godlessness increases our family homes are going to be of immense importance, because in a materialistic society, with the atmosphere polluted morally as it is, we need to have citadels of Christian fresh air throughout the whole of our land. If they are not there, then young and old will gather elsewhere. It was a wistful man who said he went to a pub, not to drink but to find some congenial company he could not have in his own home.

On every level of society, right through from the plight of the aged to the rebellion of youth, there is evidence that something has gone wrong. Family life is disintegrating, and there are good grounds for believing that there is in fact a deliberate attack on family life and family loyalty. A great deal of contemporary philosophy, grounded in facile God-rejecting humanism with its effect on the atmosphere of society, is deliberately designed to break up families. Atheistic political philosophy works very hard to make the family secondary to the state. Contemporary secular philosophy works to make the principle of individualism dominant so that "I", "my", "me" and "mine" are the issues that over-ride all other considerations. Think, for example, of some of the activities of the Council for Civil Liberties. They seem to be very selective as to who is to have the liberty. The same seems to be true about some of the pronouncements of the European Court of Human Rights. So often the claiming of liberties and rights without qualification requires some-one else to be denied.

This is the world in which we live. The situation should alarm us whichever way we look at it. We can think of it in terms of the immorality and marital unfaithfulness of parents, or the revolt of youth, or the devaluing of the institution of mar-riage leading to the disintegration of family life. The effect on the nation is seen in terms of people not knowing who they are, to whom they belong, or what is their identity. There are children who have started with one set of parents, who have then had a different set of parents, and then a different set again! This happens because people demand their liberty. They marry, then get di-vorced, to remarry as often as they like. There is nothing in the law of the land to prevent it, and we end up with a confused and lost generation, not only of children and teenagers, but of adults, who really do not know who they are, what they want or what their lives are for. Such confusion and aimlessness are a recipe for disaster.

Of course, we could say that it is the material-ism of the nation that has affected the family, and the breakdown of the family that has led to the revolt of youth. We should note that the television "soap operas" are mostly set in the context of family squabbles, family disintegration, family jealousy, family hatred and marriage infidelity. Watching or reading this kind of thing over and over again, people's minds and emotions are being conditioned until they begin to accept that this is normal. It may be normal for fallen human nature, but it is not normal in the purpose and plan of God; and therefore we have the Fifth Commandment, "Honour your father and your mother." We need God to rule in our homes and families so that there is mutual respect, love and loyalty, with all our relationships under His control. There has to be the right blend of authority, submission, co-operation and mutual respect.

But there is a difficulty in making responsible relationships within the family. This is a fact of experience which cannot be evaded, and we get near the point of this commandment when we consider human nature. It is the Biblical doctrine of man that must determine the pattern and examine the validity of our social theories. What then is the doctrine of human nature? It is fallen; it is disordered and defective.

Therefore, human nature being what it is, there will always be a conflict between rights and duties; and if a mere vote is taken, rights will always win because people are self-centred. There will always be a conflict between satisfaction and responsibility, and again, if a vote is taken satisfaction will win. By nature we are more interested in what we can get than what we ought to do. But there will not only be conflict, there will be confusion in human nature and in all its relationships, because man is quite incapable of discerning or deciding what fulfilment really is.

It is clear from the world in which we live that people have little knowledge of how to build a happy and healthful society, and the problem is simply one of human nature. It is God who changes us, who makes us new creatures in Christ Jesus, and that is the work of His sovereign, saving grace. It is all of God, it is not of man. The leopard cannot change his spots, and human nature cannot change itself. It has to be changed. It was an honest old man who, looking back over his years, wondered how it would be if he had his life over again. Then he acknowledged with a sigh that, being what he was, he would no doubt do the same things again. The glory of the gospel of Jesus Christ is that our human natures can be changed, integrated and empowered. But for this we need both God's grace and God's law which stand guard over us not only before but also after our conversion, to check our innate tendency towards transgression.

This commandment to honour father and

mother is important in the church when we consider it as a family. In society there is a tendency to separate people into groups according to age, skills, education and "class", and even in the church this worldly pattern tends to operate. Rigid division is a denial of the whole concept of family. To have a congregation which includes the whole range of ages from quite young children right up to the seventies and eighties, coming from all backgrounds and all gathering together for worship, is not only a thrill, it is a biblical pattern. You cannot have a family made up solely of teenagers. You need the parents, you need the grandparents, and you need the babies.

This concept of the church of God as being essentially a family is something that is of tremendous importance, and the dividing up of groups and ages can have a variety of bad effects. It means, amongst other things, that in the question of advice young people tend to go to their own age group rather than to the older and more experienced.

When we move into the realm of ministry, children become conditioned by visual aids. People want to *see* things rather than to *hear* them; to have them presented rather than to have to think them through. We do not apply this in an absolute sense because at times a visual aid can be helpful, but when the visual replaces the spoken word of instruction it is not good. The real issue is what people learn.

When we go on to consider the issues of Christian responsibility and duty, the pattern of dividing the age groups instead of keeping the congregation together as a family causes us to expect too little of our young people. Perhaps even in the domestic situation we have erred in doing too much for our young people instead of teaching them that all the many things that have to be done have to be shared in the doing of them. For a considerable number of years society has idolised the young. But the young do not stay young. You are a teenager for a very limited time, and if being a teenager means pleasure with no duties, you tend not to be disposed to become an adult nor to accept adult responsibility.

If society has idolised the young, so have churches, even to the point that in many churches the older generation gets forgotten. But often it was the older generation that held the church together in grim days of decline so that there would still be a church to which the young people could come. The older generation would admit that they and their work have been far from perfect, but many worked tremendously hard, at great personal sacrifice, to make sure that there was a biblical church to which the next generation could come.

If we are to have a church in the future we need to honour father and mother in the sense of recognising and following the true biblical and spiritual principles and practices of those who have gone before us: those who over many years have proved their worth. It is easy for the young, with their natural enthusiasm and vitality to be impatient with an older generation and to feel the old are slow and not progressive. Sometimes that is true, and older people must not lapse into the "we have always done it this way" attitude. But young enthusiasm can be very short-lived and some of the older generation have been at it a long time. They have stuck to it. Some young folk need to spare a thought for the fact that every day since they were born their parents have prayed for them. Honour your father and your mother for that alone!

And we apply the commandment not only humanly but spiritually. It is moving to read Paul saying in 1 Corinthians 4:15, "You may have many instructors, but only one father." He says to these Corinthian Christians who were so critical of their one-time minister, "I was the one who brought you to faith in Jesus Christ." Under God, Paul was the instrument of their conversion and, having brought them to the birth in Christ, he could say he was their father.

To turn to a more personal level: increasingly

the old get forgotten. I was visiting in the geriatric ward of a hospital on one occasion. I know there are many problems, including lack of money, but as I drove home my heart was saying, "Lord, I hope I never end up like that!" Right round the room each chair was actually touching the chair next to it. All these old people, in various stages of decline and sickness, were just sitting there side by side, looking so blank. Should it be so in a civilised society? I am not railing against any particular government, but is society healthy if it treats its old people so? I remember a situation in the early days of my ministry when the old mother of the family ended up in the institution which was by then a geriatric hospital but which all old Glasgow people regarded as "The Poor's House". She had a married son who could get a bus from his home right to the hospital gates, but he never once visited his mother. He simply forgot her.

Recall the devastating words Jesus spoke to the religious Pharisees in Mark 7:9-13:

"You have a fine way of rejecting the commandment of God, in order to keep your tradition! For Moses said, 'Honour your father and your mother;' and 'He who speaks evil of father or mother, let him surely die;' but you say, 'If a man tells his father or mother, 'What you would have gained from me is Corban' (that is, given to God) then you no longer permit him to do anything for his father or mother, thus making void the word of God through your tradition which you hand on."

Do you see what they were doing? They knew perfectly well the commandment "Honour your father and your mother," but that meant parting with their money. So they went to the Temple and perhaps signed a form "dedicating" their money to God. People nowadays do something similar when they sing, "Take my silver and my gold, not a mite would I withhold." Of course, the people Jesus spoke of did not actually hand over all their money to the Temple. That would be taking religion a bit far! But it was "dedicated". Parents might be in need but the son said, "Father, Mother, I would be willing to help you, and you know that the Lord has been good to me and provided for me, but I have dedicated all I have to the Lord. I cannot give it to you." That is hypocrisy! That is what Jesus said. Perhaps we would never do that, but do we dodge responsibility?

Think of the Commandment from a slightly different angle. A father can be so absorbed in business and in making money that wife and children can be neglected. A father or mother can be so involved in Christian activity (not the same as Christian service), that family are neglected. A prominent evangelical man was speaking at a conference, about being over-busy and he said with a laugh, but looking sad at the same time, that his teenage son wrote to him, "Dear Father, do you think it will be possible some time soon for me to make an appointment to see you? There is something I would like to talk about." The company laughed. But then we looked at the man's face and we looked at our own hearts and we wondered!

It is difficult to honour father and mother if father and mother are not the kind of people who should be honoured. We can have people who are so committed to so many things that their church-life and their family are neglected. A mother, too, can be so absorbed in her career that she has really no time for her children. It may not be career but social involvement. I can recall one woman who said, "For as long as I can remember, my mother's life has been organised round her bridge parties." How do you *honour* a father or a mother like that? You still love them.

Apply the truth to young people. Is it not true that young people can be so full of their own ploys (not necessarily bad things) that home is really just a place for bed and breakfast or for getting the laundry done, or as a source of money, or some other kind of convenience? Do we see how easily "self" can become dominant?

Whether we are speaking of the human family

or the spiritual family, honour your father and your mother, because you are in their debt. You cannot, and you must not, cast off the older people. To be honest, sometimes they can be so wilful and so domineering that it is almost impossible to cope with them. They "rule the roost", refusing to recognise that their children, whether teenage or in their twenties, thirties, forties, fifties or even sixties, need a life of their own. This, I believe, is the fruit of wrong attitudes and actions in the past. If parents do not "honour" their children, giving them the right to be individuals with a life of their own, as their age and capacities warrant, how can children honour their parents? It is not for nothing that Paul warns fathers (and mothers) not to provoke their children (Ephesians 6:4).

To honour is not the same as to obey in everything. Sometimes, for various reasons, parents can be wrong, and yielding to parents in a situation like that will confirm them in their wrongness. That would not be honouring them. The same issue arises when we are faced with the question of loyalty to God or loyalty to parents. We must put God first. We are not to hide our light. We are to let our light shine. But letting our light shine does not mean in any sense that we have to throw the lamp at people! Sometimes younger folk would have won their parents to Christ if they had not accosted them with the

Gospel so roughly and rudely. There is something about a steady shining light that eventually dispels the darkness and wins the day.

Honour your father and your mother, because God commands it, with a sense of love and a sense of value, a sense of respect and a sense of glad duty. Never forget duty. Taking a rightful share in household chores and doing so with a glad and natural spirit is a great witness. It is one way of honouring parents.

There is a story in Grimm's Fairy Tales concerning a very efficient home where the old grandfather was a bit of a problem at meal-times. His hands were shaky and he tended to spill things on the table. The housewife decided that in her well-run house this was just not to be allowed and the old man was put into the kitchen to have his meals. He got his food, not out of good china, but from cheap dishes. Then one day the old man broke one of these cheap dishes and spilt the food on the floor. More than once he did this and again the housewife was indignant. This kind of thing just could not be tolerated and the old man was told that, if he was going to eat like an animal, then he would be fed like an animal. They got a dish like a small trough and his food was put into that. The story goes on to say that this couple had one child. They thought the world of their only child, and they were intrigued one day watching him making something. When they asked what he was doing the child said, "I'm making a trough so that I can feed *you* when you are old!" The old man was taken back, and reinstated to the family. His manifest limitations did not seem to be so important after all.

Think of the debt we all owe to others, those who provided when we were incapable of providing for ourselves. Think of the struggles others had to bring us through our early years humanly and spiritually. When we are aware of the faults and failures of our parents, whether human parents or spiritual ones, have we any idea of the times that they battled with their own complications, and won the battles?

This honouring of father and mother does not deny independence. It is one thing to say to a three-year-old or a ten-year-old, "Do what your father tells you." But when the offspring is sixteen or twenty or more, we do not treat him or her like a child! Nor should we humiliate young people, either in private or in public, with gleeful stories of things that they did when they were children. That can almost destroy a youngster. When the young folk are grown up and married, do not try to keep them children. If we do such things how can they honour us as parents?

This magnificent word "honour", so absolute yet so truly gracious, allows for growth and for stages of development in relationships. It is often because relationships between parents and children are not encouraged to develop that there comes the situation in which there is no communication. It may be a painful thing to accept but parents must recognise that they are training their offspring to be independent. It is the ultimate test of a good parent that when a child comes to an age for independence he or she is capable of being independent, and of being so without a sense of guilt. You can see, portrayed in television family sagas, a tyrant mother in the process of destroying her son's marriage by the kind of comment, "If that's what you want to do, if your mother doesn't matter...". That is blackmail!

But children must also see in this commandment that their independence is not, and must never be made, an excuse for neglect of parents.

The commandment is unconditional, but it is not legalistic. Nor is it blind. A child is not required to look at a disastrous parent and say, "You are a very good parent. I would not have you otherwise." That would be dishonesty. But our knowledge is limited and some of us know very little about our parents. The word "honour" is not to be understood merely in the sense of duty. It has to do with love. You cannot honour someone simply out of a sense of duty even though duty shows respect. There must be love, and love has to be shown because love has been received. It is not an unfair burden that we should be commanded to love because we are recipients of such wealth of love from God and from man.

Look at Ephesians 6:1-4 to see advice on how to balance family relationships. People say, "Yes, and the ideal is realised in Christian family life." It should be. But in fact it is often the opposite, because too many Christian parents live in fear lest their children will not turn out right and so reflect on the parents' spirituality. Of course if the dominant note of the family is fear, the end product may well be the very thing dreaded. What if the child is a Christian and the parent is not? Honour your father and your mother. After all, who should make the best son or daughter, the Christian or the non-Christian?

It all comes back in the end to love, and to the love of God which is shed abroad in our hearts by the Holy Spirit. Children, honour your father and your mother as the Lord your God commanded you, that your days may be prolonged and that it may go well with you in the land which the Lord your God gives you. But parents, make it possible for your children to honour you with gladness of heart. Amongst other things, parents (not merely mothers, far too many fathers contract out of responsibility in bringing up their children) recognise that bringing up children is in itself a glorious fulfilment, humanly and spiritually. It is a career far more rich and far more rewarding than the business of making cash and spending it; more rewarding even than personal career fulfilment. It is far-reaching and fundamentally creative. Who knows what part our children will play in the demanding days that lie ahead of us?

This is a commandment full of life and full of possibilities. It brings the love of God right to the very heart of our relationships, and when we heed it and come to God in the yielding of our hearts that we might do His will, then I believe we enter into life, not least that kind of life which makes a Christian home and a Christian family like the very threshold of Heaven itself. At the same time it is an outpost in the battlefield of spiritual warfare.

Children and parents, look to God and look to the future. The commandment is a word of grace and life.

THE
SIXTH COMMANDMENT
No Killing

In this series of studies we have dealt with the commandments on as broad a basis as possible. We have tried to avoid ending up with a mere set of rules which could make us feel satisfied if we kept them. Rather we have sought to compel ourselves to think through the implications of the commandments. It is particularly important to do this with the one that says, "You shall not kill." Most of the translations of the Bible render it in these words, but the New English Bible says, "You shall do no murder." This may seem at first to clarify the meaning, but in fact it does not help a great deal because we must then consider how we define "murder"; and indeed we must consider how we define "kill".

It would be easy to take the Sixth Commandment as it is expressed in a single short verse of Scripture and, on the basis of its apparently simplistic statement, to denounce both capital punishment and all forms of war, requiring all Christians to be pacifists, and then calling, in the name of Christ, for unilateral disarmament. Whether this would lead to peace, prosperity, fulfilment and godliness is very open to question. After all, there was no threat of nuclear warfare when Cain murdered Abel. There was no such threat when, at the time of Noah, the world went rotten to such an extent that God regretted that He had made man upon the face of the earth. There was no threat of "Star Wars" when the activities of the cities we call Sodom and Gomorrah brought a committee of enquiry down from Heaven. What we have to recognise in all our studies in the commandments is that it is human nature, with all its bias towards and capacity for evil, that is the real problem. In the Garden of Eden, circumstances, economics and atmosphere were all perfect, and yet man chose wrongly. It is in the context of the fallenness and perversity of human nature that we have all these commandments. God, recognising our capacity for going wrong, gives His ten words of grace, one of which is, "You shall not kill."

But we cannot take this commandment in an absolute and simplistic sense because if we say, "You shall not kill," and leave it like that, we would be required to adopt the attitude of Buddhists and others whose regard for what they call "the sacredness of life" is extreme. Missionaries have told us what happened in a certain village with a dog sick with rabies. It was a danger to the village and to the children playing there: what did these Buddhists do? They would not kill the animal because life is sacred. They captured the rabid dog, carted it away, and let it loose in another village. *They* were now safe and *they* had not killed! This is the complication of taking "You shall not kill" in a simplistic and an absolute sense. Some Christians have tried to adopt this attitude, including the late Albert Schweitzer, a man of considerable character, who did a great work. But such was his attitude with regard to life being sacred and therefore not to be taken that he would not even allow insects in his hospital to be killed. If we protect *all* life, we can, by doing so, endanger human life.

There is also the danger that, absorbing the spirit of the world, we can hold human life too cheaply. Death had no place in God's original creation; it came as a result of sin. Go back in thought to the Garden of Eden. Do not try to go back in practice as some misguided people try to do. They have the attitude, "We don't like the world as it is. We are going to make a private world where there are none of these bad things that we dislike, things that make our lives unhappy." They are trying to recreate the Garden of Eden in this present world order. But this is escapism, for it is totally impossible for man to make a Garden of

Eden, a paradise of experience, because the essential problem of all that we mean by evil is in man and only secondarily in his circumstances.

In the Garden of Eden, at the instigation of the tempter, man chose self rather than God, and man became aware at the very moment of his rebellion of a standard of comparison between good and evil. He also introduced Death. As Romans 5:12 says, "Sin came into the world through one man and death through sin." What he did not find in his fall was any possible means or power of control over his new situation. He knew of good and evil but also knew that he was now in a situation where he had no control over either, nor any real control over the essential conflict that there was between them. Resulting from what happened in the Garden of Eden there is an unbroken train of consequences which no human power can stop.

Right from the dawn of human history there was embedded in the conscience of fallen man an awareness of his inability and his incapacity. He himself had created a situation which he could no longer control, a situation into which *he* had introduced the element of evil. There lay before man the inevitable complications of the entail of sin, one sin leading to another, elaborations and counter-elaborations, involvement and further involvement, until we have the hideous tangle that we now call human history. But right from the beginning there was also the Word of God which declared in that situation the promise of a Saviour that was to come.

The outflow from the Garden of Eden is not just a situation that no human power can control but also one that no evil power can control. To put it as bluntly as possible, I believe that even the Devil himself is aware of the fact that the situation is out of hand. It is an awareness of this incompetence on the part of the persons and powers of evil that explains something of the frenzy of the world, a frenzy that is becoming more intense as the bafflement of experience becomes more immediate and dark. The awareness of being trapped is becoming more a factor of world experience, and out of this comes the fear that leads not only to vandalism but to people getting pleasure from causing destruction and pain of all kinds. You can, in measure, understand brutality used in order to steal a bag of money. But when someone assaults a complete stranger just for the sake of doing it, this is baffling. While you can understand some men and women, battered and bruised by life's experience, indulging in the grotesque and hideous cruelty that we read of in the newspapers, when you read of this kind of thing being perpetrated by boys and girls as young as twelve or eleven years of age, you begin to see a situation that is out of human control and becoming increasingly a situation of irrational frenzy.

All the evil we have described, culminating in death, comes as a result of sin. In a situation like this and standing over it there is the Lord God Almighty, ruling in righteousness, declaring His commandment, "Thou shalt not kill."

Death is the ultimate insult to all that we mean by human nature. Death is an enemy (1 Corinthians 15:26) and a devastating contradiction. You watch your children being born, developing and coming to manhood or womanhood. You watch all their capacities beginning to flower and you begin to see something of the magnificence of the image of God in which man was once created, just as you can see grandeur in some of the ruined castles in the Highlands. Although they are ruins you can still see the lineaments of grandeur and from that you can picture what that castle was in the days of its glory. So it is with human nature, fallen and vitiated though it is. You see something of the dignity of humanity and then cutting across it all comes this ghastly spectre of death. It is indeed tragedy.

Man resents war, suffering and death but he does not repent. As experience presses in upon him and he becomes more and more aware of the fact that he can neither control nor escape from that situation which the fall has brought to pass, he begins to get angry and rebellious. This attitude is shown in the story of the dying thief crucified along with our Lord. Remember the blasphemy of his utterances, so typical of mankind in its resentment against God. The wicked thief turned and said to Jesus, "If you are the Son of God, save yourself and us." He meant, "If you are a real God worth believing in, do something. Get us off the hook." It was the other condemned criminal who stated the truth. "This man Jesus has done nothing wrong. We die justly. We die because of what we are and what we have done, and you just want to escape the consequences of the wrong you have done." One man facing execution had no thoughts of right or wrong, only a spirit of rebellion against circumstances and a desire to escape the consequences of his own actions, regarding which he had no sense of repentance. The other man acknowledged the rightness and the justice of his final punishment.

It is easy to be unreasonable. Some people, in the name of humanity, cry out against war; but at the same time they claim the right to free and unfettered self-indulgent action in the moral realm, to live as they please, to do what they want, to strike, steal, hurt and murder, without being called to account or punished. The issue in the commandment is far deeper than that of war or pacifism or capital punishment. To concentrate on these issues alone could be sheer escapism.

Think of the words of our Lord Jesus Christ who speaks plainly of a wrong attitude of anger and of devaluation of another as being linked with killing:

"You have heard that it was said to the men of old, 'You shall not kill; and whoever kills shall be liable to judgment.' But I say to you that everyone who is angry with his brother" (some translations have "without cause") "shall be liable to judgment; whoever insults his brother shall be liable to the council, and whoever says, 'You fool' shall be liable to the hell of fire" (Matthew 5:21,22).

Jesus does not do away with the commandment, "You shall not kill." He makes the standard higher and He drives the principle deeper. He reminds us that these things of which we have been speaking, these attitudes, hatreds and contempts, lead to consequences of punishment and judgment, not only in this life but in the world to come in Hell.

When we ponder Jesus' words about the consequences and the punishment of sin, it helps to look further at this Sixth Commandment. While Exodus 20:13 says, "You shall not kill," if we go on to Exodus 21:12, we read:

"Whoever strikes a man so that he dies shall be put to death."

How do we square these two verses? We must hold them together and not interpret one without the other. If we read further in Exodus 21:13-14 we find this elaboration and qualification:

> "But if he did not lie in wait for him, but God let him fall into his hand, then I will appoint for you a place to which he may flee. But if a man wilfully attacks another to kill him treacherously, you shall take him from my altar, that he may die."

That is paying the price for his sin of killing. There is a distinction made between deliberate killing, "murder", and what we now call "manslaughter". The former merits death. When we look carefully at Exodus 21:17 we see that the crime or the sin of cursing parents, whatever that may mean, is also regarded as a serious contradiction of God's order. If we read through that chapter, and some of the succeeding ones, we find that sometimes the punishment is death.

When we go right through Old Testament history we read the story of the conquering of the land of Canaan and find, at the command of God, whole cities being put under judgment. How do we square this with "Thou shalt not kill" if we take it in a simplistic sense? Some people try to dodge the issue by saying that this is the Old Testament and we now live in the New Testament age.

In answer to that, there are three things to be

said. The first is that the whole Bible speaks of the activity of God in two aspects: salvation and judgment. Evil is not free, never was free, and it will be brought to judgment both now and in the world to come. We need to be reminded, even in the evangelical church, that there is a Hell as well as a Heaven. We tend to forget this. We must face the issues of eternity. Not all evil is brought to judgment and punishment in this world, but it will come to judgment in the world to come. In the whole matter of salvation and judgment God is the active agent. It is God who says, "The soul that sins, it shall die."

It is God who likewise forbids everything that comes into the category of personal revenge. Whether we quote it from Deuteronomy or from Romans 12, God says, "Avenge not yourselves; vengeance is mine; I will repay." It is in the context of God's judgment of evil that we see the wonder of His work of salvation. The Cross of Christ which declares salvation for sinners is the place where sin met its full judgment and its price was paid in death.

The second thing to be said is in relation to the words of Jesus, "You have heard that it was said, 'An eye for an eye, and a tooth for a tooth'" (Matthew 5:38). In the Old Testament law this principle was enacted not to require retribution but to limit human reaction and human revenge.

It was *only* an eye for an eye, *only* a tooth for a tooth. If someone sinned against you and stepped on your toe, all that you were entitled to do on the basis of justice was to stamp on his toe with exactly the same pressure as your toe suffered. That is what the law was saying: no savage, extreme, personal revenge. Revenge is not God's way; God's way is justice. But justice can sometimes be very grim.

The third thing is that some of the sternest words in the New Testament about judgment and Hell were spoken by our Lord Jesus Christ. Sometimes He was extremely stern as, for example, when "Gentle Jesus" took a whip in His hands and cleansed the Temple because men in their perversity and greed had distorted both the house of God and the message of God's grace. Of course, only Jesus had the right to act in that way. For the rest of us, God says, "Avenge not yourself" (Romans 12:19). This links up closely with the commandment, "You shall not kill."

It is easy to forgive people when they have not really hurt you. It is easy to be marvellously Christian then; but if someone has said or done something that really cuts you to the quick, fallen human nature reacts. Now, God recognises the fallenness of human nature and sets barriers of grace for our protection. You shall not kill.

When this commandment is mentioned

people still insist on referring to the Sermon on the Mount, which is in fact a most disturbing sermon. We referred to Matthew 5:38-39:

> "You have heard that it was said, 'An eye for an eye and a tooth for a tooth.' But I say to you, 'Do not resist one who is evil. But if anyone strikes you on the right cheek, turn to him the other also.' "

Does this require us to be pacifists, and in a literal sense does it require us *never* to resist evil? Of course not. If you come across someone selling your child drugs, would you say, "The Sermon on the Mount says, 'Resist not evil' "? Would you stand by and let it happen? Have you no sense of responsibility? That cannot be the application of "Resist not evil". What did Jesus mean when He spoke of turning the other cheek? Professor William Barclay in his book on the Ten Commandments points out that if you are right-handed it is difficult and unnatural to strike someone on the right cheek: you would strike the left cheek. Jesus chose His words carefully. If you are right-handed and striking someone on the right cheek, it is a backward strike and you are not assaulting them but insulting them. On the basis of insult, you take it, and you do not resist. That is what Jesus did when they spoke all manner of wrong against

Him. Personal insult can be accepted, but that does not mean that we should not speak out and act against unrighteousness in society. We cannot press the word of Jesus, "Resist not evil," to an extreme. That would make nonsense of the Bible.

Both New Testament and Old Testament speak of justice. God is never indifferent to wrong. Consider Romans 13:3, 4:

> "Rulers are not a terror to good conduct, but to bad. Would you have no fear of him who is in authority? Then do what is good, and you will receive his approval, for he is God's servant for your good. But if you do wrong, be afraid, for he does not bear the sword (of justice) in vain; he is the servant of God to execute his wrath on the wrongdoer."

That means in our broad thinking on this Sixth Commandment we must refuse to allow it to be used to demolish the question of punishment in general and capital punishment in particular. On this theme Professor William Barclay makes a sweeping statement which is typical of those who generalise and formulate opinions regardless of clear statements in Scripture. He says, "All Christian teaching about punishment declares that punishment must be designed for the reformation of the wrongdoer." That is a personal opinion. It is not what the Bible says. His opinion regarding punishment must be rejected on other grounds also because, if the objective of punishment is to reform the wrongdoer, or for that matter to deter others, then it gives governments the right to "treat" people (as some governments do) to change their attitudes, to reform them by medical and psychiatric treatment so that they will no longer say things or do things that are inconvenient for the state. Punishment is not justifiable simply to make someone conform or to deter other wrongdoers. If it were it would be permissible, and some might say desirable, to punish an innocent man merely on the ground of suspicion if it was thought that this might have a desirable effect. That is immoral. The only justification for punishment is that it is *deserved*. In other words, the only justification is the element of retribution.

I believe the Bible teaches that certain crimes deserve and require the forfeiture of life. This is not a contradiction of the Sixth Commandment, nor is it a slipping back into barbarism. It is standing on biblical authority.

I respect those who have different views on the subjects of the death penalty, pacifism and unilateral disarmament. But we are required to think biblically. We have to recognise that nuclear power; all that we mean by the ecological crisis; all that we mean by space exploration (or for that matter, space invasion); and all the other horrific

119

possibilities that may come, are all inescapable facts of experience. All these things are part of the world that man has made. We may resent it, but it is our own doing, whether by our own actions or by our own neglect. We cannot control the fallen world that man's sin has brought down. We cannot escape the present consequences, nor can we escape the final consequences, which consequences are death and judgment.

"It is appointed unto men once to die, but after this the judgment" (Hebrews 9:27 AV).

We cannot put the clock back and start again. We cannot stop the world and get off.

We may try to bury our heads in the sand and pretend that the problems are not there. If people feel that is the limit of their responsible involvement in world affairs then they had better bury their heads in the sand. It is not a very positive contribution. Nor is it God's way. He says, "You shall not kill", and this does not simply mean that we must refrain from murder and unlawful killing. It means that we must defend life; not only our own life but our neighbour's life. The trouble with so many of us, because of our basic self-motivation and preoccupation with our own experience, is that by and large we just don't want to know about other people, their needs and their problems. Like the hypocrites in the story of the Good Samaritan, we pass by on the other side. Consider well Jesus' words about those who do nothing in Matthew 25:31-46.

There is a devastating inconsistency in human thinking and at times we need to expose it. There is, for example, an understandable outcry in our own day against killing animals, but there is much less outcry with regard to killing babies. We try to avoid the grimness by referring to "foetuses". Think of the statistics with regard to abortion and think of the human lives these statistics represent.

We also need to recognise that we kill each other by careless driving, and drunk-driving. Where do we stand with regard to drink? We are part of a society that is tolerant of drunk-driving, and we speak plaintively about people's right to drink if they so wish. We always focus on "rights", that is our rights, not the other person's. But how many personalities, especially those of children, are so brutalised by drunkenness and selfishness that they are virtually killed? A drunken driver is disqualified; the victim is killed. God says, "You shall not kill."

As we study this commandment honestly we have to apply it more widely still and recognise that some attitudes and practices we adopt can drive someone to a slow death. We can destroy a person without actually having them declared clinically dead. We build a society which is based on creating desire, demand and expectation, and in the process we make it impossible for such desires to be fulfilled. The result is that people are driven to cracking point and are destroyed. We create a way of life in which there is such a pressure on some people that they grasp almost desperately for any apparent escape, whether it is adults taking drugs or youngsters sniffing glue. There is a lot of killing done by drug-pushers and also by drink-pushers, and one of the most significant developments in our contemporary society is the increase in the number of "off-sales" licences up and down the country. As we allow this to happen, seldom if ever taking the trouble to write a letter of protest with regard to the possible opening of an off-licence in the area in which we live, by our lack of action to prevent the killing process being set in motion, how do *we* stand with regard to this commandment about not killing? There are marriages being killed by many different processes and we may help to prevent such a "death" not least by showing what Christian marriage can be.

We may protest at these applications of the commandment by saying, as Cain did, "Am I my brother's keeper?" We may ask, "What can we do?" I could answer, "What have you tried to do?" There are those who will do anything because of money. Are not Christians called to be salt and light?

It is easy to point the finger at the big issues, as we have been doing, but, if killing is in some measure equivalent to depriving of life or destroying life, we must also consider our attitudes to those near us. Think for example, how we can work out our own ambitions and frustrations through our children, our parents and our friends. Think how we can exercise tyranny over another person by outbursts of temper, by prolonged bouts of sulking, and by a variety of processes by which we make it our business to bring that other person under our power. What are we doing? We are depriving that person of life. It is possible so to manipulate people, whether family or friends, that we leave them with no life of their own. They are not allowed to do anything on their own. They cannot make any decisions on their own. Their life has been taken from them. How then do *we* stand in relation to the commandment, "You shall not kill"?

Remember that at the heart of the Commandment there stands the sanctity of life, respect for life, and respect for personality. It is there to curb the hideous and ruthless self-will of our fallen human nature, self-will that would ride over God as well as man. The law stands with its commands and its sanctions. The world stands with its horrors pressing in upon us, and increasingly we become aware of just how helpless we are. The world to come stands waiting for us: "It *is* appointed unto men once to die and after this the judgment."

In such a world as this I can understand why people begin to say, "What shall we do to be saved?" The answer is, "Believe on the Lord Jesus Christ and you shall be saved." Look to Him, and what do you see? You see the Son of God who was delivered up to death as the Sin-bearer, to carry the judgment of sin for you and for me. When you look to Christ and see Him thus, and you come in faith to Him, you begin to see that no development of the human situation, however frightening, is outwith the control of God. You begin to see that God is already judging the world. You begin to come to terms with the commandment that says you shall not kill, you shall do nothing to harm life, and you will do everything in your power to defend it, no matter the cost.

THE
SEVENTH COMMANDMENT
No Adultery

The Seventh Commandment is expressed in five simple straightforward words: You shall not commit adultery (Exodus 20:14). Our studies have revealed the commandments to be not only precepts of righteousness and prohibitions of evil, but also words of sheer grace: words given by God to keep men and women from destroying themselves because of the natural tendency of fallen human nature. We cannot emphasise too often that man is a fallen creature and he lives with his fallen nature in a fallen world. Therefore man, left to himself, will destroy himself and everybody else, and everything else with which he comes in contact. It is for this reason that we are neither embarrassed by nor afraid of the tremendous negatives in the Ten Commandments. It is God who knows human nature through and through who says again and again, "You shall not."

We have also discovered that built into the negative aspect there is a positive one. For example the commandment "You shall not kill" not only forbids the taking of life but is a requirement to guard life, to honour life, and to take our stand to oppose everything that would harm life. This positive as well as negative aspect is also present in the Seventh Commandment. You shall *not* commit adultery, and the wider implication of that is that we are to see to it, before God, that we live lives that are pure and good and true. In our study we shall take adultery to include all breaches of chastity and purity, inside or outside the marriage bond. We apply the commandment on the broad basis of all that we mean by immorality.

Mere abstention from actual acts of immorality is not enough; also forbidden is that kind of life that sails as near the wind as possible, tempting both self and others, while taking care always to be in a position to say, "But I didn't do it." That is the attitude that our Lord Jesus Christ challenges and denounces in the Sermon on the Mount where He says:

> "You have heard that it was said, 'You shall not commit adultery.' But I say to you that everyone who looks at a woman lustfully has already committed adultery with her in his heart" (Matthew 5:27, 28).

This phrase that Jesus uses, "looking lustfully," does not refer to what one commentator calls "natural erotic impulse." It refers rather to the calculated attitude, the deliberate and provocative looking of those who keep themselves from action only because of fear of consequences. And remember, there are consequences both in this world and in the world to come. Paul warned the Ephesians (5:5, 6):

> "Be sure of this, that no immoral or impure man, or one who is covetous (that is, an idolater), has any inheritance in the kingdom of Christ and of God. Let no one deceive you with empty words, for it is because of these things that the wrath of God comes upon the sons of disobedience."

This is not an easy commandment to study. In our consideration many subjects have to be by-passed with a mere mention, for example the question as to what constitutes marriage. Is it the conjugal act, or the legal contract, or the religious contract? That raises another question, which also must be by-passed. What do we mean by divorce? What is the place of divorce in the context of all that we mean by Christian marriage? In Christian marriage we say the words from Scripture:

> "Whom therefore God has joined together let no man put asunder."

In that realm, what is the place, if any, for the remarriage of those who have been divorced?

This leads to yet another question, and our concern is to encourage thought. Is there a case, as C S Lewis suggests in *Mere Christianity*, for two kinds of marriage, one for Christians who believe in God, who name the name of Jesus Christ and claim to live by the Word of God, and another kind of marriage for those who make no profession of faith and who may not even believe in God? Is there a case for one kind of marriage that is constituted before God, and another kind of marriage that is merely contracted before the State? Or is all marriage to be seen as it is seen in the Scripture narrative of the Garden of Eden: one man and one woman in the will of God for life? There is a thrill in using the words in a Christian marriage ceremony when first the bridegroom and then the bride are asked to make their vows, the final words of which are, "And keep thee only unto her (or him) so long as you both shall live." It is a magnificent question. When I look round my congregation and see lots of married couples, I know full well that in their heart of hearts they are saying, "Yes, we would say it again."

There is yet another hard question. If we see no difficulty in allowing Christian marriage for someone who has lived a very bad life morally, but who has come to Christ in repentance and has now been assured of forgiveness (even though he may have regrets for the rest of his life), do we then go on to say that "breakdown of marriage" is the only failure and the only sin for which there is no forgiveness and no fresh start?

These questions are hard to answer and we should never give answers too quickly. They deserve careful thought if we are to discern Christian standards and maintain them in secular society.

In all these issues and in all our consideration of them in the light of Scripture, we must start by taking the highest ground. We must always start there. It is clear from both the Old and New Testaments that God's plan, pattern and standard, right from the dawn of creation, was one man and one woman for life. This was one of the principles built into the order of creation right from the very beginning. Jesus said:

> "Have you not read that he who made them from the beginning made them male and female, and said, 'For this reason a man shall leave his father and mother and be joined to his wife, and the two shall become one'? So they are no longer two but one. What therefore God has joined together, let no man put asunder" (Matthew 19:4-6).

The Bible records that the disciples of our Lord

Jesus Christ were shaken by His enunciation of this principle and standard. But when we start considering the whole question of marriage, from creation right through the Bible, we discover that long before the Ten Commandments were given adultery was regarded as a sin against God. Think of how, in the story of Joseph, when the wicked wife of Potiphar tried to trap him, he cried out, "Far be it from me to sin against God!" The standard was clear even though the Ten Commandments had not yet been given. In the story of Abraham even earlier, we find that among pagans, and they were cultured pagans, the king of Egypt was horrified that someone who was supposed to be a man of God was double-dealing and had concealed the fact that a beautiful woman was his wife, with the result that Pharaoh nearly took her as his wife. Pharaoh of Egypt was shocked by a man who put the sanctity of his marriage in peril. He rebuked Abraham also for putting him in peril by nearly involving him in adultery.

We must think about these things in order that we might recognise that in the whole realm of moral misconduct we put ourselves and others in a very serious and dangerous position. Taking "adultery" in the widest sense of including any sexual immorality, we must recognise that such behaviour is a contradiction of God's order. Because this is so, those who indulge in it introduce confusion into God's order of things in the world. They introduce confusion into their own lives, into the lives of those with whom they are involved, and they introduce confusion and a spirit of pollution into the whole of society. Sexual sin is not a light thing!

People say that it is not the "bit of paper" that constitutes marriage, it is love and a stable relationship. But a relationship that begins and continues by ignoring God's institution of marriage is a potential disaster. Anyone who has been involved in pastoral care of others knows the hurt that comes to many because this great commandment has been ignored. Think of the demolishing of all that we call family life. Think of children who do not really know to whom they belong. There was a film made about a situation where two lots of parents got divorced and all four remarried. They tried to make it into a comedy because it was so confusing. The children did not really know who they were supposed to call "mother" and "father". In real life that is tragedy not comedy. Think of our present-day society with the attack on marriage itself. We read in newspapers of people saying, "I want the right to have a child." They do not want to get married and have no intention of getting married, certainly not to the one who fathers the child. They want the right to have a child, and the interests of the child are secondary. We read of men and women whom we could describe as "not the kind to marry" who say they want a child. They want to adopt a child but deny the right of the child to have two parents. This is the confusion into which we have got.

Statistics keep changing but it is good for us to consider them even though they are frightening. Think of the number of marriages that end in divorce. Think of the number of abortions. Think of the percentage of children conceived before marriage.

Society is geared (and the producers of television, magazines and paperbacks will have a lot to answer for on the Day of Judgment) to propagate the idea that immorality, adultery and homosexual practices are normal, an accepted thing, and just part of life. It is a lie. It is also a lie when people say or infer that "everybody does it." Young people need to be told this is just not true. It is a lie of the Devil to lead you away from God, away from life, into the brokenness and the misery of living a life that is a contradiction of God's love. Let all be aware of it: there are consequences. Because of these things the wrath of God comes upon the children of disobedience.

To be realistic, we must recognise that in the world in which we live when we say, "You shall not commit adultery," many people respond by asking, "Why not?" Having made this arrogant response they often go on with a spirit of rebellion to say, "Who are you, and what right have you to interfere with what I do? What right have you to criticise my action? What right have you in the name of your God, in whom we do not believe, and in the name of the Bible, which we do not recognise and consider to be out-of-date, to deny us our fulfilment?"

It is clear that God's ordinances are devalued. Some of the most indignant are the adulterers and the immoral. There was a time when people living together outwith marriage made a calculated attempt to conceal the fact. They were aware that the opinion of society would be against them. That is no longer the case. A whole section of the community saw no reason at all why a high-ranking government minister who was an adulterer should not continue in office, dealing with and looking after the affairs of the nation. Such was public opinion.

But not only is marriage as God's ordinance devalued: the whole area of personal and sexual relationships has been reduced to the level of desire and inclination. Think, for example, of some of the implications of the "Gillick Case", as it was called. Think of the furore, the reaction and the resentment. Think of how, as on other occasions, the Family Planning Association said with such an appearance of righteousness, "We are not here to set standards. We are here to help." What they were actually doing was setting the standard of "there are no standards." On their own confession they are concerned only with easing or preventing certain consequences. Such is the distance society has moved from the Seventh Commandment. Think of the report at one year's General Assembly of the Church of Scotland by the Social and Moral Welfare Board. Think of the reaction and the misunderstanding when some fairly radical biblical things were said with regard to the issues of abortion. Since then I have had cause to discuss matters with some members of the committee which produced that report and they astonished me with revelations from statistics showing that current legislation is not improving the situation. It is not preventing illegal abortions. It is not preventing many of the moral and social consequences.

What we need to say very clearly is that nothing that is contrary to God's law can ever be of benefit to society or to human life.

Consider the statements of Scripture: for example, Paul's words in Colossians 3:5,6.

"Put to death therefore what is earthly in you: immorality, impurity, passion, evil desire, and covetousness, which is idolatry. On account of these the wrath of God is coming."

Of course, society does not believe in the wrath of God. Society does not believe that God does anything.

But the Bible says very plainly that as a result of certain things men and women do, as a result of the way they live their lives, God is angry, and His positive action of wrath and displeasure comes upon society. We read this same message in Ephesians 5:6, to which we referred earlier. We have the same command in 1 Corinthians 6:18. In two words we have a great call and exhortation: "Shun immorality."

It is not something that can remain outside yourself. It involves you far more deeply than you realise. Immorality has a price. For your own sake and for society's sake, keep the commandment. That is the call of Scripture.

When people are challenged they may say, "We are deeply in love." The answer to that is very simple. If the person is married to another, you have no *right* to be in love. People protest and say their feelings are so strong that what they do must be right. It cannot be right if it breaks God's law. Let me illustrate. Have you heard people saying, "I was so angry with him I could have killed him"? They had strong feelings, but they did not do it. Feelings have to be controlled. And they *can* be controlled. Have we not been in the position where we felt very strongly, "I would just love to tell him what I think of him!"? But we do not! We had the powerful feelings, but they were controlled. It is no excuse to say, "We did not mean to do it but our feelings were so strong." We must be honest with ourselves and with others. When someone says with heat and passion, "I love you," what they often mean is, "I love myself and I want you." That is not love; it is desire.

People tend to confuse these feelings but they are two very different things. Society is hungry for love, but that is not the same as gratification of desire. Desire is essentially an animal instinct, and as Professor William Barclay points out, the mark of true humanity in man and woman is self-control. He goes on to make the obvious, but very penetrating, comment that immorality is simply a case of demanding the privileges without the responsibilities. It does two things. It dishonours and devalues the other person, because it is not a real relationship, nor is it the fruit of a relationship that has grown. The second thing is that in violation of the commandment of God, when immorality takes place there is no real hope of the two people then getting to know each other as true people. The whole relationship is exclusively focused on the physical, and is thereby narrowed down.

True love is not selfish, nor will it ever demand its expression in a way that will grieve, hurt, hinder or dishonour the loved one. Love gives value to another. Love will always respect the dignity of personality. A man's love should never adopt any attitude or indulge in any action that will cause the blush of shame or the smear of guilt to rest upon the girl whom he loves. Love ultimately dies for the good of the loved one, and that is the word of the Cross. Love is willing to die rather than harm or even soil the loved one. For your loved one's sake, keep the commandment. Do so also for the Lord's sake.

Look at 1 Corinthians 6:15-20:

"Do you not know that your bodies are members of Christ? Shall I therefore take the members of Christ and make them members of a prostitute? Never! Do you not know that he who joins himself to a prostitute becomes one body with her? For, as it is written, 'The two shall become one.' But he who is united to the Lord becomes one spirit with him. Shun immorality. Every other sin which a man commits is outside the body; but the immoral man sins against his own body. Do you not know that your body is a temple of the Holy Spirit within you, which you have from God? You are not your own; you were bought with a price. So glorify God in your body."

No one should be discouraged by this call for a

way of life that is pleasing to God. He knows how we are made. Our hearts cry out for love. That is part of human nature. We need to be loved, and we need to be able to give our love. But when the heart cries out for love, does not the Word of God say: "Behold, what manner of love the Father hath bestowed upon us" (1 John 3:1 AV).

It is the kind of love that sets value upon us, a value above price. It is the kind of love that gives us dignity, wholeness and purpose. Take time to think deeply about God's love for you; take time to tell Him of your love for Him. We also need to share that love by showing care to each other within the greater context of the saving love and law of God in Jesus Christ.

In our own lives there is hope in the Gospel. God broke into the deplorable situation of human sin. That is what the Cross is all about. God came down and comes near to you with all the potency of His redeeming love. This God has condemned sin in the flesh by the death and resurrection of Jesus Christ, robbing sin of its power; and by the Eternal Spirit, through Jesus Christ, He is able to give us a new nature, a new life-stream, in which the potency of sin has been broken forever. Think of the hymn:

A heart in every thought renewed,
    And full of love divine,

Perfect and right and pure and good,
    A copy, Lord, of thine. (Wesley)

That is the heart that we need and that is the heart Christ came to give.

But what of those who have sinned grievously? What of those who carry a burden of regret and shame? There is a hymn that says:

Convince us of our sin,
 Then lead to Jesus' blood,
 And to our wondering view reveal
 The secret love of God. (Hart)

Where better can we end our study in this commandment than with the story from John 8 of the woman who was taken in adultery? There is no mention of the guilty man in the story and we leave him aside. The other men, self-righteous and religious, dragged the woman, without compassion, into the presence of the Son of God. That poor wretched soul heard the Son of God saying, "Neither do I condemn you, go and sin no more." When Paul wrote to the Corinthians he mentioned a long list of ugly words and he said to the Corinthians, "and such were some of you, but you were washed" (1 Corinthians 6:11). Think too of the promise, "Though your sins are like scarlet they shall be as white as snow" (Isaiah 1:18).

But some may say anxiously, "It is since I became a Christian that I have sinned and fallen." What does the Bible say?

"If we confess our sins, he is faithful and just, and will forgive our sins and cleanse us from all unrighteousness" (1 John 1:9).

It is not only forgiveness but a new heart, a new life, a new sanctification and a new satisfaction, and all of it is in Jesus Christ who loved us and gave Himself for us. We began with the commandment of the law and we end with the grace of the Gospel.

THE
EIGHTH COMMANDMENT
No Stealing

The commandment stated in Exodus 20:15 is very short, a mere few words, "You shall not steal." Some may feel the impact better if we reduce it to: God says, "No stealing." It is as blunt as that.

In practice, what do the words "no stealing" mean? You would not snatch an old lady's handbag, but would you fill in your Income Tax form wrongly? If you were selling a car, aware of the fact that it had a strange, significant sound in the engine and that there were problems of extensive rust which you had covered up, would you keep quiet about these things? You want to get a price greater than the actual value of the car. Is that stealing? Do we say stealing from the old lady is somehow different from stealing from the Inland Revenue or in the second-hand car market? Are we allowed to make such distinctions?

The Commandments are difficult to preach on because the application of them is so wide and comprehensive. Sermons on the Commandments are difficult to read honestly because they are so challenging to, and so interfering with, our personal choices, inclinations and whole way of life. The Commandments simply will not allow us to live our lives the way we please. They insist that we live, both positively and negatively, in a way that will please God. The Ten Commandments, one after the other, put the sword to self-interest, which is the basic drive of fallen human nature. It is clear in Scripture right from the story of the Garden of Eden that man's motivation has been, and still is, personal fulfilment and personal ambition. These are the things that so easily, often without our noticing it, become the dominant and conditioning factors of the way that we live: my ambitions; what I want; my fulfilment; my "rights", whether justified or not. This self-interest motivation operates regardless of God; and when the situation arises in which what God says seems to frustrate my freedom and my rights, then God must go.

We have emphasised repeatedly that these commandments are words of grace, standing over against man to prevent him destroying himself and others. This is certainly true with regard to this commandment, "no stealing", because at the heart of stealing is self. Self is greedy. *I* must have what *I* regard as *my* entitlement, regardless of what it does to others or what it deprives others of. This "self" can become greedy to the point of murder. Our selfishness can become so total that we are prepared to do down everyone and everything in order to get what we want.

Take an example from the story of David, a man of God. On one occasion he stayed at home when his army had the right to his leadership in battle. They deserved his leadership but he deprived them of it. While he stayed at home, on a particular afternoon his eyes fell upon a beautiful woman, Bathsheba. Forgetful of God and His laws, thinking only of his own desire, he took her. He stole her from her rightful husband. Then, in order to keep her, he arranged, with considerable difficulty, the murder of her husband. But we read in 2 Samuel 11:27, "The thing that David had done displeased the Lord," and He sent the prophet Nathan to him, to confront him with the facts of what he had done and to say, "Why have you despised the word of the Lord, to do what is evil in his sight?" (2 Samuel 12:9).

How then are we to learn from this commandment to guard ourselves from falling into the danger of stealing? We must recognise first of all that it affirms the right of property. It makes plain that there are things people may rightly regard as theirs and no one else has the right to take them. Now, there are only three ways of having property: by working for it, by gift (including inheritance), or by theft. If you have what you have because you have worked for it, or because it has been freely and gladly given to you by another, you are in the clear. But if you have it by any other means there is a question-mark as to your entitlement.

This commandment has no meaning unless there are things which belong rightly to the individual, or to an organisation. There are times when ownership is in doubt and is debated furiously in courts. There can be no conviction for stealing unless it is clear to whom a thing belongs, and that has to be decided first.

We could raise questions about the actions of some governments. The state is not God and is bound by the law of God as much as the individual. Some people seem to think the state is more important than anything or anybody else, and so demand a loyalty to the state that is totally unreasonable. The state is bound and restricted by the Ten Commandments the same as everybody else, and the state has no right to steal.

There is a telling illustration of this in 1 Kings 21. It concerns King Ahab, the head of the state, and Naboth, who owned a vineyard. The king (who represents the state) coveted the man's vineyard and sought to negotiate for its purchase. Naboth refused on the ground that it was the family inheritance, and to preserve the name of the family he declined to part with it. The king, aided and abetted by his wife Jezebel, the most wicked woman in all the Bible, arranged things so that Naboth was murdered and the state took over the vineyard. It was stolen. But when you read through towards the end of that chapter you become aware of the fact that God was angry and pronounced a grim judgment upon the state, Ahab and Jezebel, for this thing that they did. They had stolen what, in the providence of God, rightfully belonged to another man, and they paid the penalty.

In the business of people having a right to property, there are those who say that the right should be limited to small ownership. They say that it is unfair that some have so much and others have so little. But where do we draw the line? We usually draw it at the level we are at ourselves. Those who have as much as we have (or less) are in the clear, but people who have more than that we tend to question. Such a position is hardly tenable. In Scripture, New Testament as well as Old Testament, we find ownership amongst some of the great believers. Barnabas, for example, was a landowner. He sold all his lands and gave the money to the church for the proclamation of the Gospel (Acts 4:36,37). It was a tremendous action. Peter and some of the other disciples owned fishing boats of considerable size. James and John left their father with the boats and later Peter was able to go back fishing (John 21:3). Then there were Ananias and his wife Sapphira (Acts 5:1-11). They came to a bad end, but it was not because they owned property, nor because they gave only half of the proceeds to the work of God, keeping the other half to themselves; they were judged by God because they made a deliberate decision to be hypocrites and to tell lies. They went to Peter and the apostles and they claimed to be giving the total proceeds. They wanted to be thought as spiritual as Barnabas, who had done that very thing. Their sin was not that they kept something of their own property to themselves; their sin was that they lied deliberately to God and to man, seeking to steal reputation to which they had no entitlement.

When we follow this matter of "the right to have or to own" through the New Testament, we find that very soon after the Day of Pentecost there came into operation what could be called a simplified form of "communism". The believers sold their possessions, and they had all things in common. No one lacked anything. It sounds marvellous until we find a few chapters further on, in a matter of months rather than years, that the whole Christian community was in difficult financial straits. This caused friction, division and tension. Disruption arose from what was held in common. They could not agree as to what were fair shares. Their communalism had problems. Later on, the problems increased in spite of wise administration, and the other churches had to send financial help to the Christians in Jerusalem. A better system of mutual benefit was needed. Having everything in common was not laid down as a continuing principle for the church.

There is a right to have and to own. But we must be totally clear that, in whatever form we have anything, it is held in our possession under God. It is not ours in a total sense and never can be. It has all to be stewarded for God, and this applies whether it is financial wealth, or position, or personality. It is difficult to say which of these is hardest to handle! But all that we have has to be seen in terms of opportunity to serve. This is the only safety for wealth of any kind. Remember that Jesus said in Luke 18:24, "How hard it is for those who have riches to enter the Kingdom of God!"

Why is it so difficult for rich people to enter the Kingdom? It is because what we have can very easily cloud our faith and steal our trust, and we forget how totally dependent we are upon God. Recall the story that Jesus told of the rich man in Luke 12:16-21. There is no suggestion that he was a bad man morally, or corrupt in his business life. He was efficient, very hard working, and he built barns, and he built more barns. The fellow had a real problem: the more successful he was, the more successful he became, and his riches took up all his time, thought and energy. Then God spoke and said, as it were, "You foolish man, this night your soul will be required of you. You may have made your will. You may have all the provision made for your family and for what is going to happen to your money. But this night your soul will be required of you."

That is a disturbing thought, because on the night our soul is required of us we stand before God. I believe that God will say, "What did you do with all that I gave you? How did you use it? How did you steward it? Did you do it faithfully as belonging to Me? Did you seek My mind and My will? Did you always remember that you yourself are not your own but a servant of the most high God? Or did you take it all and use it for yourself?" That is stealing.

Turning from our own rights, under God, to ownership, we must look now at the question of whether we would ever infringe the rights of others. It is easy to fall into the snare of manipulating and adjusting the law to fit in with our own cultural or emotional convictions. We protest that we would not break into someone's house. We would not shoplift. We would not pick pockets. But, if we saw someone else doing these things, would we take action? We must not only obey the commandment "no stealing", we have to do everything in our power to stop others stealing and to prevent stealing becoming a way of life.

No form of words must be allowed to cloud the issue. You hear it said that certain things are "accepted business practice". That is quite irrelevant. If the action, however slight, is dishonest, that is stealing. It is wrong in the sight of God, and no man or woman, believer or unbeliever, is entitled to do it. If we say that this kind of radical attitude would cause a mighty disruption in the business and commercial world, then let the disruption come. It will be a more constructive disruption than working to rule and unofficial strikes. We need to be very practical about this whole business. There is a tendency for people in responsible positions to say with regard to pilfering, which is stealing, "You have just got to turn a blind eye." Where does it say in the Bible that we should turn a blind eye? Exodus 23:2 says, "You shall not follow a multitude to do evil."

There was a television documentary in which a mother, living in a very tough area of the city, had reported her own son to the police for theft. The interviewer was puzzled and expressed his surprise, but the woman explained that her son had broken into a poor widow's house and that, in her code of behaviour, was not right. She had no hesitation in reporting her own son to the police and he was arrested. She saw the importance of not stealing, but it was only in a limited context. When the interviewer asked, "Supposing your son had broken into one of the big stores in town and stolen from there, would you have reported that?" Her answer was immediate, "Oh no, that's different." But we are not allowed to be selective or to set our own standards.

In the chapters following the giving of the commandments in Exodus there are many specific applications of "No stealing." In Exodus 22:1,3 we read:

> "If a man steals an ox or a sheep, and kills it or sells it, he shall pay five oxen for an ox, and four sheep for a sheep... He shall make restitution; if he has nothing, then he shall be sold for his theft."

Restitution is an element in justice that has been nearly forgotten in contemporary society. Later in that chapter there is reference to the situation in which a man lets his beast loose and it feeds in another man's field. He must make restitution from the best in his own field, because his beast has stolen from another man's pasture. The issue there is one of carelessness that leads to another person's hurt. That is a form of stealing.

The chapter goes on to speak of a situation in which someone has come asking for a loan and his garment has been taken as a pledge of security:

> "If ever you take your neighbour's garment in pledge, you shall restore it to him before the sun goes down; for that is his only covering; it is his mantle for his body; in what else shall he sleep?" (Exodus 22:26,27)

We are told there that human concern takes priority over our rights, and when we fail in that way we are stealing. The Scriptures are plain and radical. Turn to Leviticus 19:13:

> "You shall not oppress your neighbour or rob him. The wages of a hired servant shall not remain with you all night until the morning."

In these days the workers were paid at the end of each day, and it was as they collected their wages that they were able to go and buy the food that they needed for their family to eat that evening and the next morning. If the employer was careless, or ruthless, making excuses about being busy and not able to have the money ready, God says that was stealing. The working man, with a heavy heart, had to go home to his family and tell them there was no food because his wages were kept back. Nowadays employers can steal from workers by lower wages and poorer conditions than are right. At the same time the workers can steal in terms of time-keeping, shoddy work and pilfering.

Note that the beginning of the verse in Leviticus speaks about "oppressing", or "robbing", and there are many ways in which we do this without involving money.

Think, for example, of a noisy party that goes on until the early hours of the morning. That is oppressing your neighbour. That is stealing from your neighbour his rightful peace.

It is the same with regard to car parking. Pressed for time one day, I was looking for a parking place in the centre of the town. Near the shop where I had one call to make there was a space. Just as I drove into it I noticed that it was marked, "For disabled drivers only". It was a temptation: I would not have been long. But suppose I had parked there and within a minute of my going away there had come along in a car someone virtually crippled, hoping for that place. Suppose he had to go a long way before he found somewhere else to park and then, with every joint of his body aching, had to hobble back to where he wanted to go. Would I not have stood guilty before God, having stolen that person's rightful parking place? I am glad to say I didn't steal it!

More solemnly, we must apply the commandment in the realm of breaking the speed limit and careless or dangerous driving, because by that means we steal from others on the road their rightful safety, and possibly their future.

We could multiply illustrations. In the Book of Deuteronomy 22:1 it says that if your brother's ox goes astray you must not withhold your help; it is his right. You drop what you are doing, take your brother's beast and see that it goes safely home. Your brother has a right to expect that from you, and if you do not do it you are stealing. In modern terms, when we see something wrong we should do what we can to put it right. That is very reasonable.

But in Exodus 23:4 we are told that if we see our *enemy's* ox straying we have to act in the same way. The standard is high. We must not take from anybody that which he has a right to expect. Has our enemy a right? Since when did Christians work on the basis of rights? Does not Scripture say that God commended His love toward us in that while we were yet sinners Christ died for us? (Romans 5:8).

There are so many other ways of stealing. Think of Shakespeare's words:

"Who steals my purse steals trash;
'tis something, nothing;
...   .
But he that filches from me my good name
Robs me of that which not enriches him
And makes me poor indeed."

Are we always careful about what we say about others? You can steal a person's character by gossip. You can steal a man's reputation by criticism and contempt. You can steal someone's peace. It is very easily done. A brief sentence, or even a phrase sometimes, just as you leave a person, can send him home to lie awake half the night. You have stolen his peace.

You can isolate a person by stealing his friends. A child can come home from school very sad, perhaps even weeping, saying, "So and so has stolen my friend." But it is not only in the school playground that it goes on. Have you ever stolen someone's friend, taking that friend for yourself?

You can attach a person so much to yourself emotionally that you steal from them their own personality. You deny them the friendship of others, and so keep them to yourself, that you prevent them from having the privilege, the pleasure and the profit of being of service to others. That is stealing.

Just as over-intense friendship can be stealing, so can self-centredness and ignoring others. You can sometimes say rather heartlessly, "My friendship and help are there if he wants it." But the person in question may be so hurt and so needy that he is incapable of coming to you to ask. By not going to him you have denied him the help he needed. You can be so absorbed with yourself and with your own particular friends that you never really do anything for anyone.

That leads on to the very serious question in Malachi 3:8,9: "Will a man rob God? Yet you are robbing me. But you say, 'How are we robbing thee?' In your tithes and offerings. You are cursed with a curse, for you are robbing me; the whole nation of you."

Would anyone steal from God? The answer is "Yes". Keeping back from God what is His by right; reluctance in service; absence from duty: all these are stealing from God. We must be even more searchingly honest than that and recognise that such is the subtlety and the powerful dynamic of "self", that it is possible for what we call Christian service (perhaps we should say Christian "activity") to be self-fulfilling rather than God-glorifying. We do it because we like doing it; we find fulfilment in doing it; we are happy doing it. Note how egocentric it is. But Christian service that is motivated basically by self is neither honouring nor acceptable to God. It is all too easy to use the Christian platform, pulpit or arena to make a name for self rather than for Christ. In all kinds of Christian activity and groups we can gather people in attachment and loyalty to ourselves rather than to Christ. But if through the preaching of the Word of God and the proclamation of the glorious Gospel we draw people to ourselves, we are stealing from God. It is God who has paid the price for the redemption of these people. They are His by blood-bought right, and if we draw people to ourselves then we are stealing from Him.

Not only are we stealing from God when we do that, we are stealing from people, because we are keeping them from the God that they need. If we make people dependent on us for advice, counsel, care and pastoring, doing everything for them, they will develop the habit of coming to us. But people don't need us! They need God. It is a fact of experience that the whole area of Christian service, especially the kind of service that puts us onto a platform of any kind, giving us publicity, is mightily dangerous. This is one reason, I believe, why God hedges in the lives of those who are called to be ministers of the Word with a whole variety of difficulties, complications and restrictions. It is to keep them safe from allowing self to obtrude, because that would lead to stealing from God and from men.

The commandment "You shall not steal" is of much wider application than might at first be seen. It applies to the whole realm of duty. If we fail to fulfil our Christian responsibility in duties that we have freely and gladly accepted, for example in church membership, then we are both stealing from God and stealing from God's church. We can even give ourselves to Christian work and activity to the point of exhaustion, but if we are not where we should be we are stealing from God. Who are you neglecting? Who are you taking for granted?

Another danger is that we can give our time and our money to the Lord in a way that steals from others the time and the money that should be given to them. If a minister throws himself into the work of his ministry with enthusiasm, gladness and dedication, and does so to such an extent that he neglects his wife and children, he has stolen from them what is their God-given right. The principle applies not only to ministers but to everybody. Stories could be told of how Christian marriages have broken, and how some children of Christian families have been poisoned against God and the Gospel, because there has been stolen from the wife or the children that which belongs to them by right.

The trouble is that even as Christians, born of God, with the very life of God within us by the Holy Spirit, we allow the shadow of gruesome self to intrude. When this happens and self begins to rule life, personality, family, friendships and congregation, there is introduced a grating disorder, a disease, an unpleasantness, a spirit of wrongness, in which atmosphere we break the commandments. In many ways we become thieves.

"Thou shalt not steal."

Recall the prophecy of Malachi: "Will a man rob God?" Will we, Christians though we claim ourselves to be, degenerate to the level of being common thieves in respect of God? Yes - when we allow the ravages of self to overshadow our lives, to interfere with our fellowship and relationship with others; when we allow self to deny our fellowship with God, and self-will to come between the glorious intentions of God and the fulfilment of these intentions. We are robbing God in that we are denying God His right, by sovereign grace, through the death and resurrection of Jesus Christ, to see in us His image perfectly restored.

We do well to say:

Take my life, and let it be
Consecrated, Lord, to Thee... (Havergal)

or, put in the words of Scripture:

"I beseech you therefore, brethren, by the mercies of God, that ye present your bodies a living sacrifice, holy, acceptable unto God, which is your reasonable service" (Romans 12:1 AV).

Anything less, is to steal from God.

THE
NINTH COMMANDMENT
No Lying

When we study the Commandments in sequence we begin to realise that the standard for Christian behaviour is totally comprehensive and absolutely uncompromising. In the negative commandments, each of which has a positive aspect, not a single part of human individual or social experience is allowed to escape the scrutiny and the challenge of God. But we must not see in these commandments merely the challenge, because repeated challenge can debilitate and leave us disheartened and demoralised. To use the commandments only as a rod of rebuke and condemnation is to misuse them; we have also to learn that the law of God is impregnated with the grace of God. The grace of God in the law stands over against man's natural capacity for degeneration.

We have to grasp this truth with regard to ourselves, society, and the whole wide world. By nature man has an inbuilt capacity for sin but in the thunder of the law, which can be frightening at times, God challenges man's natural degeneration, and points him to his true manhood and dignity. For ourselves and for the sake of others these prohibitions of the law stand sentry over the dignity of man made in the image of God.

We have pointed out with regard to the negative commandments how comprehensive this guard duty of the grace of God is. Man's person is safeguarded by "Thou shalt not kill." The family is safeguarded by "Thou shalt not commit adultery." The right of property is guarded by "Thou shalt not steal." Now the important theme of man's honour is safeguarded by this commandment, "Thou shalt not bear false witness against thy neighbour."

We must examine our thinking before it ever issues in conversation lest we do despite to the basic and fundamental honour of one of our fellow men or women by bearing false witness against them, either by what we say or refuse to say. What tremendous damage can be done when we speak wrongly about others. If we blight or cast a shadow on a man's honour, God will be angry. A man's dignity, a man's character and a man's peace are to be preserved. Consider these words of our Lord Jesus Christ in Matthew 12:36,37:

> "I tell you, on the day of judgment men will render account for every careless word they utter; for by your words you will be justified, and by your words you will be condemned."

That means on the great Day of Judgment, Almighty God will ask, "Why did you say that about that person, knowing you were bearing false witness?" It is a solemn thought. Our words are a good indication of our nature, and speech can often be a true indication of spiritual condition.

We must be careful because human nature being what it is, and the Devil being who he is, there is always the possibility, not because of major steps but because of a succession of minute steps of false witness, that we lose our whole sense of right and wrong, our sense of truth and error.

This is the danger of all that we call gossip. Take time to consider how much there is in the New Testament, particularly in the Epistle of James (3:1-10), with regard to letting no corrupt communication proceed out of our mouths (Ephesians 4:29 AV; Colossians 3:8). We had posters during the war declaring that "Careless talk costs lives." If we indulge in false witness, contrary to the safeguarding commandment of the law of God, we will end up in what can only be called a condition of inconsistency, and with a tendency to manipulate situations, facts and people for our own justification and our own ends. Never forget that some of the sternest words spoken by Jesus were addressed to those who were guilty of false witness, acting a part, playing the spiritual hypocrite.

Sometimes a false impression can be created without a word being spoken. Think of it this way: in a given situation one person says to another, "By the way, have you heard about...?" "No." "Oh well then, best leave it like that." And this is said in such a way and in such a tone that it gives the impression that there must be something terrible to be told.

Think of situations in which one speaking to another may say, perhaps bringing the conversation to an end, but with deliberateness, "Perhaps I know him better than you." And one person goes away with a whole lot of question-marks, "I wonder what that means? I wonder what's behind it?"

Think of a situation in which one can say to another, and you can imagine the tone, the look on the face and the attitude, "No smoke without a fire!" There may in actual fact be no "fire" at all, but the impression has been given and the suspicion has been kindled that something is not altogether as it ought to be; we have borne false witness.

We can do it even with two little words, usually accompanied by a cynical smile, when we say, "Ah yes..." That is all it needs, and suspicions are roused. People sometimes do it to a minister when they say, "If you had heard what so-and-so was saying about you after the service last Sunday..."

Many a minister has gone home to a sleepless

night, being vulnerable at the end of a day's preaching, because some foolish Christian has babbled words that were unnecessary, though perhaps intentional. There may not have been anything significant in what the original person said about the minister after the service, perhaps it was false witness.

In Deuteronomy it is made clear that in a legal case judgment could not be reached on the strength of one witness:

> "A single witness shall not prevail against a man for any crime or for any wrong in connection with any offence that he has committed; only on the evidence of two witnesses, or of three witnesses, shall a charge be sustained. If a malicious witness rises against any man to accuse him of wrongdoing, then both parties to the dispute shall appear before the Lord, before the priests and the judges who are in office in those days; the judges shall inquire diligently, and if the witness is a false witness and has accused his brother falsely, then you shall do to him as he had meant to do to his brother; so you shall purge the evil from the midst of you" (Deuteronomy 19:15-19).

Perjury is still regarded as a very serious offence in the courts of law in our own land. That passage in Deuteronomy indicates how solemnly the business of false witness has to be regarded and how sternly it has to be dealt with, so that the whole of society can be warned. In Deuteronomy 17:7 the witnesses were required to be the executioners. That would bring home to false witnesses the consequences of their words.

This business of false witness refers particularly to testimony in court, but it also applies to truth in our business dealings, to speech as a whole, and, of course, to gossip. The commandment tells us to be sure that what we say is true so that we are willing to stand publicly by what we have said. We are to speak the truth, the whole truth and nothing but the truth. That sounds straightforward. But it is not as simple as it sounds, because we are all apt to be prejudiced. When we describe something that has happened, while not wanting to tell lies, we tend to give our account in a way that shows us in a good light, and in a way that is slanted against the person that we do not like. Speaking the truth is not an easy thing, because when we are influenced by self-interest, we are apt to choose words that suggest that we are in the right.

An illustration of this is given by Professor William Barclay. He tells of a judge who on one occasion said, "If I were to believe the evidence of both sides I would have to come to the conclusion that there had been a head-on collision between two cars each of which was stationary on its own side of the road." We may smile but it is very difficult when there is an accident to give a totally unbiased account of what we consider to be the facts if we ourselves are involved.

We are also prone to exaggeration. A minister was counselling a lady. They knelt to pray together and the lady, confessing her sins, was saying, "Lord, you know that I have this weakness for exaggerating things." At that, the minister broke into the prayer and said, "Call it sin, not weakness." When we tell a story we can make certain aspects of it appear bigger than is true, and this is bearing false witness. In the matter of speaking the truth, the whole truth and nothing but the truth, we can easily lapse into the snare of manipulation. We present the facts in a way calculated to get the listener to do what we want, or to have a higher opinion of us than is right. We manipulate the truth to make the other person go with us rather than with another.

This kind of manipulation is, to my mind, the essence of the advertising industry. (Include in the advertising industry all that we mean by the "pop music" industry, where the whole set-up is geared to make people part with their money.) Advertisers do not pay many thousands of pounds to tell us the plain truth about their product. That is not their objective. Their objective is to constrain us to buy their product rather than someone else's. There is tremendous skill in the advertising business, particularly in advertisements for alcohol. The suggestions made by advertisements are, by and large, a matter of bearing false witness. Drink this, drink that, or drink the other, and you will get on; you will be witty; you will get the beautiful girl; you will get a big yacht on the Mediterranean; drink this and all these things will come to you. It is not confined to drink: use this toothpaste, that scent or that aftershave and all the things that you have ever dreamed about will just come your way. It is not true. The makers may say that the implied claims are not meant to be taken literally, but if advertisements did not influence people's choice they would soon be dropped.

More seriously, the truth of the matter is that we are being manipulated right, left and centre. We are being conditioned to believe there are things without which we simply cannot live, that everybody has them and so must we. It is not true! The truth is that it is quite astonishing just how many things there are that we can do without and not be any the worse. If we could get that into our minds and hearts, what a release of money there would be for the missionary work of the Gospel to the ends of the earth!

We have the same kind of manipulation of the truth in books and plays where sex is portrayed as a thing in itself, as the way of life. It is not! But a whole generation has been subjected to this false witness, not least the assumption that causes many to think, believe and feel that "everybody does it." That is a lie, and it is so obviously a lie that society should see through it, but it does not seem to. I will never forget, as long as I live, counselling a young girl. She sat in the vestry with tears rolling down her cheeks and said to me, "But Mr Philip, he said he loved me." Yes, he said that, but it was false witness to gain his own end. Actions speak louder than words.

When we speak like this we begin to see that in the matter of false witness we are into the realm of what is devilish. After all, did not our Lord Jesus say that the Devil is a liar from the beginning? The Devil is also expert at making lies sound and appear like the truth.

Think of false teaching about God, both in sects and also within the church. A whole company of men and women, up and down our dear land, parade themselves as apostles of Christ and they are not. They may speak with the voice of men and of angels but their inspiration is the inspiration of Hell, and they are doing untold damage to many Christians and to the truth of the Gospel. Look at 2 Corinthians 11:13-15:

"Such men are false apostles, deceitful work-

men, disguising themselves as apostles of Christ.
And no wonder, for even Satan disguises himself
as an angel of light. So it is not strange if his
servants also disguise themselves as servants of
righteousness."

There is much in both the Old and New Testaments about false prophets and false miracles.
We must not be gullible and assume that all
miracles are necessarily worked by God. In the
early chapters of Exodus, when in the name of
God Moses did mighty things, Pharaoh's magicians may have said, "That's all right. We can do
that as well," and they did (Exodus 7:8-13). Consider 1 Timothy 4:1:

"Now the Spirit expressly says that in later times
some will depart from the faith by giving heed to
deceitful spirits and doctrines of demons."

That verse often comes to mind with regard to the
contemporary religious situation within our land.
Deceiving spirits bear false witness and lead many
away from God and away from truth into error
and ultimately into darkness. We have to be much
on guard. We must refuse to be taken in.

One reason why devilish false witnesses have
such influence is because words are very powerful. We see this also in the realm of politics. I, for
one, begin to wonder just who can be believed and

what can be believed. There are so many hidden factors in the life of a politician, who has to be very careful what he says, because always in the background there is the next election. Politicians have to be careful because they want to guarantee that people will still vote for them. It is little wonder that our country is in the state that it is. We should ask ourselves if the politicians say the same kind of things when they are in office as when they are in opposition. Try to remember what has been said in the past. Do politicians now slant what they said formerly, in order to achieve their end? But if they manipulate the truth in order to achieve their end they are guilty of false witness.

Many cannot remember the 1939-45 war and Goebbels, the German minister of propaganda, but some of us do still remember how he poured out torrents of words, because he was aware of how effective false witness was in undermining the morale of an enemy nation. Hitler cynically said, "Tell people a lie often enough and they will believe it."

Do you think that is an exaggeration? The lie need not be strident; it can be very quiet, just repeated over and over again. It may be someone meets you only once a week, but says something to you this week; next week he says it again; the week after he will say it again. He knows it is false, he knows his motives are wrong, but in the end you may very well believe it. This worries me.

Think, in the realm of secondary school education, of the philosophy of evolution. I am not talking about the scientific *theory* of evolution, which is a different thing; scientific theories have to be examined on the basis of being scientific theories. What I am referring to is the philosophy assumed and built on the basis of a theory which is being taught as fact. Watch some of the nature programmes on television and see how the commentary suggests that everyone knows that evolution is the explanation of creation. This is having an effect. People assume that the theory has been proved and that everyone thinks it is fact. But remember, God says, "You shall not bear false witness."

We have considered deliberate lying in various different fields but we must also apply this commandment to those times when we are suddenly tempted to "twist the truth". There is an evil dynamic in false witness and we need to recognise that it can take us completely by surprise. We find ourselves unexpectedly in a crisis, the kind we think has to be resolved immediately to allow life to go on, and in a moment we speak. What we say gets us off the hook, but it is false witness. We find the same kind of danger in time of strain, when, scarcely knowing what we are doing and yet not being sufficiently guarded against it by our walk with God, something is said which we do not deny, some opportunity is given and we speak negatively or positively what is essentially false witness, and there is set in motion a sequence of events which we can no longer control. The same happens in times of reaction, when we have gone through some trying experience and feel jangled, with our nerves a bit raw. In reaction of anger, bitterness, resentment or self-pity we speak about someone and, sowing seeds of doubt about their person and character, we bear false witness. James 3:5 says:

> "So the tongue is a little member and boasts of great things. How great a forest is set ablaze by a small fire!"

How searching God's Word is: with the tongue we bless God and we curse men; these things ought not so to be. We need God's help to control our tongues.

When we are asked questions about people or situations and it is clear the questioner has no right to or need for the information, what should we do? There is no need to give the information, nor to give false information. The best thing to do is to say to the questioner (who may be a gossip), "Why do you want to know?" There is seldom a satisfactory answer given. If they persist they can be told plainly that we do not talk about other people's concerns. We have protected someone's privacy. We have prevented false witness.

Apply the commandment to our own religious life. Consider false witness in terms of the words that were spoken by God through the prophet Isaiah in chapter 29:13:

> "And the Lord said: Because this people draw near with their mouth and honour me with their lips, while their hearts are far from me..."

God looks down from Heaven, He considers and He says, "These people are using the right words; everything they say is biblical; it is sound doctrine; it is spiritual truth. They are not only saying all the right things, they are doing the right things. But one important thing is missing: their *hearts* are far from Me."

In one sense we can bear as much false witness as we like, but God will not be taken in. Think of how Jesus challenged the Pharisees with hypocrisy. What does hypocrisy really mean? It is a word derived from the theatre, speaking of acting a part. We can give the impression that we are dedicated to God when in fact our whole life is self-motivated. God looks on the heart.

Ministers have to take the question of false witness seriously, particularly at funerals. If a minister knows full well that the person who has died had no place for Christ in his life, and lived a life that could not bear scrutiny in any sense; if he reads the words of the service committing the person's body, dust to dust, ashes to ashes, and adds the words, "in sure and certain hope of resurrection to life that is eternal," is that not false witness? The mourners will think that the minister is saying, "He has gone to Heaven." But he is bearing false witness.

I remember reading the words of an African pastor who had been in this country. He said that the spirit of universalism, the belief that everybody goes to Heaven in the end, is the main barrier to the work of the Gospel in the United Kingdom. I agree. How difficult it is when, as the minister of a parish, you are called to certain homes. What a burden it is when you are aware of no indication of faith, nor even of religion, and you hear those in the family saying, "Ah well, he is at peace now." It is not helpful to be brutal, and it is very difficult in the context of brokenness of heart to communicate that those who die unbelieving die in their sins.

This is why so often at funerals, I say the words, "Hear the word of God as it asks the question, 'If a man dies shall he live again? It is appointed unto men once to die and after this the judgment. Therefore let a man give diligence to make his salvation sure.'" You shall not bear false witness. That also means you shall bear true witness.

It is not enough to say, "I never tell lies." Good for you! But have you given people the right impression? Have you borne true witness to them? Have you told them that there is a Saviour; that there is a Hell as well as a Heaven; that we have souls that need to be saved? We must bear true witness.

We are required to speak the truth, the whole truth and nothing but the truth, but there is a time to be silent. Bearing true witness does not just mean telling the bare facts. The spirit in which the words are said also matters. People say almost triumphantly, "I just told him!" That can be sheer cruelty. I have challenged people on this level and they have replied, "What I said was true." The actual words may be true in themselves, but what of the general impression that they give? Is it strictly true? The Bible says that we are to speak the truth in love, and that love will always try to believe the best. Jesus said, "Blessed are the peacemakers."

There are three questions that we should ask ourselves: Is it true to say it? Is it necessary to say it? Is it kind to say it? Always remember that the Spirit of God in our hearts is the Spirit of truth, and when we bear false witness, in whatever way, we grieve the Holy Spirit.

Take this commandment seriously. Whole churches have been betrayed by false witness.

Characters have been assassinated by false witness. Lives have been corrupted by false witness. Do not be a hypocrite, but keep the spirit of the commandment. You shall not bear false witness. Over against that, let your light so shine before men that those who know you will see the truth and the truth will lead them to the Saviour.

THE
TENTH COMMANDMENT
No Coveting

We could express the Tenth Commandment, "You shall not covet your neighbour's house; you shall not covet your neighbour's wife, or his man-servant, or his maidservant, or his ox, or his ass, or anything that is your neighbour's" (Exodus 20:17), in twentieth-century terms and say: whether it be his wife, his car, his house, his job, or his building society bank-book, you shall not set your covetous eyes and greedy heart on anything that rightly belongs to your neighbour.

At first sight we might be tempted to think that this is merely repetitive, saying the same kind of thing as the commandments regarding adultery and stealing. But this is not so. The Tenth Commandment highlights the power and perversity of human nature in all its craving. Even if a man does none of the things prohibited in the earlier commandments there is still a problem to be dealt with, namely the inner attitude of his mind and heart. A man can burn with deep and radical covetous desire on various levels and yet never in fact take any action. Is he thereby innocent? What a man thinks in his heart, so is he (Proverbs 23:7 AV). The inner attitude of mind and heart is challenged and cautioned. This commandment should make us stop to consider what life is making us, and what we are becoming because of the way we live.

Some people, by their attitudes and motives, narrow down life and make it bitter rather than sweet for themselves and for everybody with whom they come into contact. Some seem to have all that anyone could ask for and yet stand out as being discontented and dissatisfied. They never seem to be pleased. They are so busy complaining, whether outwardly or inwardly (and I am not sure which is the more sinister), that they never seem to think of gratitude to God, or parents, or friends for what they do have. Such people do not even seem to enjoy what they have.

This was brought home to me when I visited a home where they had recently renovated the sitting-room: new fireplace, carpet, curtains, wallpaper, suite. Everything was new and it was lovely. I complimented the lady on her superb room. Instead of looking pleased she said, "Oh, but if you saw the mess the bedroom is in; I don't know when I will ever get it done." She had accomplished so much but she was not enjoying it. She was feeling no pleasure, not only because her bedroom still had to be done, but because a friend in a bigger house had managed to redecorate sitting-room, bedroom and bathroom. She was envious. She was coveting. The result was she had no pleasure in all she had. The only word to describe that lady's condition is "sad". Some people, no matter what they have, never enjoy it because they are always thinking of someone else who has something more, or something different, or something better. They concentrate on what they do not have rather than what they do have. This is a bitter spirit, and it is the kind of thing the commandment about coveting brings into focus.

A word of caution is necessary here, because the commandment does not say, "You shall not want," or "You shall not hope." There are longings that are natural and legitimate. An anonymous letter (not a nasty one) came to me. It was an article from *The Evangelical Times* about the problem of being a single woman. There were many parts underlined with great emphasis upon all the misunderstandings that married people can have about unmarried people; the glib comments that married people (even Christian ones) and parents can make to those who are not married, or who are married and do not have children. It is true that many people are tremendously insensitive about the feelings of others, and it grieves God. There is no excuse for it. I agreed with the article and had sympathy with whoever sent it, even though they seemed bitter. Life can hurt; it can be very sore. But I refer to this article in order to emphasise that it is not wrong to want to be married. It is not wrong to want to have children. It is not wrong to want to have a nice home. It is not wrong to want to have understanding relatives. It is not wrong to want to have caring friends and a satisfying job. Human nature by its very creation is ambitious. It has aspirations and capacities. It cannot be otherwise because men and women are made in the image of God, and God is a creative God. Therefore, made in the image of God, we will always have aspirations and capacities that we would like to develop in the best, fullest and truest sense.

It is right and proper that we should have these ambitions and they are not in themselves a contradiction of the commandment, "You shall not covet." After all, Paul urges us to "Covet earnestly the best gifts" (1 Corinthians 12:31 AV). Let there be a deep burning desire to be the best that we can be for God and for His Christ. There is a coveting that is not only right and permissible, but necessary. Just as *wanting* in itself is not wrong, so also there is nothing in this commandment that forbids the legitimate and rightful longings and hopes of humanity, particularly a hunger for companionship on all levels. It was God Himself who said it was not good for man to be alone. But a qualification is necessary. We must face the fact that the world in which we live is fallen, disordered and unbalanced, and therefore *all* our legitimate hopes and desires cannot be fulfilled; that can never be until there is a new order of Heaven and earth. One of the blessings of Heaven is that there will be no more pain of any kind and no unhappiness or tears. Here in this fallen world we have to live with frustrations, tensions, demands and denials, but we can address ourselves to them with very different attitudes, and this is where we begin to come to the crunch point of the commandment about coveting. Our attitude to our longings and ambitions is the heart of the matter. Are they all-important to us or does God's will for us come first?

We do not avoid coveting by adopting an attitude of grudging resignation. To do that is essentially negative: an attitude in which we are not prepared to make any kind of effort at any time, on any level, for any reason or for any objective. Someone may lament that he has no friends in the congregation. But does such a person ever try to *make* friends? If we sit back with an attitude of resignation thinking, "I'm terribly lonely and it's just not fair," our faces will get longer, our attitudes and disposition will get more and more depressing, and it will become more and more difficult for anyone to get anywhere near us to make friends with us. This attitude of resignation towards life is not only negative, it is demoralising.

Some ministers would like to be able to preach and to expound the Scriptures as competently and comprehensively as men they admire. In a right sense they covet excellence. But they only seem interested in the end result and are quite unwilling to pay the price of self-discipline and hard study. They want the reward without the work.

Sometimes people want to be or to do what God has not planned for them. This is coveting. A spirit of discontent is dangerous. We can develop an attitude of resentment against God as well as man. People say, "I don't know why this should happen to me." But an honest review of our way of life and our much sinning could reveal many reasons why a whole lot of unpleasant and nasty things should happen to us. That they have not happened is a testimony to the grace of God. But it is easy to lapse into a permanent feeling of being cheated by both man and God, a spirit of complaint, rebellion and coveting. We refuse to be content with life as it is, and we begin to long for what another has.

The alternative is to address ourselves to the complications and demands of life in a spirit of faith. That means an attitude which looks to God and trusts Him even when we cannot understand why things have to be the way they are. That is faith. We do not pretend that life is a bed of roses. There is an old hymn that says, "Now I am happy all the day," but we must not sing that glibly when we feel unhappy. If we are not happy we should not say that we are. That is bearing false witness and breaking another commandment. Instead we look to God and say, "I don't understand why my life has to be like this, but You must know and therefore I am prepared to trust You." This commandment has to do with the deepest parts of our whole life, personality, motives and relationship with God.

This is no exaggeration. Read Romans 7:7 and see that it was this commandment about coveting that eventually convicted Saul of Tarsus and showed him that he needed to be converted. Paul declared that if it had not been for the law he would not have known what sin was. He would not have understood what it was to covet if the law had not said, "You shall not covet." There is a suggestion here that Paul had gone through the Ten Commandments, one by one, and had felt he was more or less in the clear. But when he came to the very last one he was convicted and realised that he had not only a greedy spirit, but the kind of selfish ambition that was an affront to God. He not only had a greedy spirit, he had a cruel spirit and he became aware of what he was really like.

God says, "You shall not covet." This has to do with things we have no right to possess. We are not talking necessarily about bad and ugly things, we are also speaking about straightforward, honourable and good things. People say, "If they are good things why can't we have them when we want them so much?" The answer to that is simply that God has not seen fit to give these things to us. I can still recall clearly the time in my ministry when I said to God (and it was very costly) that if, in order to be a fruitful and useful servant of the Word, I had to be a bachelor all my days, I was willing to be so. I was not a "natural" bachelor. It was one of the costliest decisions that I ever had to make. In God's mercy I did not have to remain single. It worked out well but I had to wait. It is only as the years have gone by that I have been able to recognise and understand some of the reasons why the delay was necessary. At the time I had to guard my soul against coveting and complaining.

A commentator on the Ten Commandments made the point that coveting is instinctive rather than calculated or premeditated. The actual words were: "Coveting is the involuntary action of the soul towards the external object which presents itself as corresponding to the desire." Put it into different terms. There is the inner desire, there is the outward object, and when they are brought near the spark crosses the gap and the circuit is complete. Think of it in terms of the Garden of Eden. If ever a person's circumstances were ideal, Eve's were. She had a God-given partner, and what none of the rest of us have, a God-given partner in whom there were no flaws or faults! Everything she could possibly need was there. Her circumstances were all that could be desired. But what do we read? She saw that the fruit of the tree was good for food; she saw that it was a delight to the eyes; she thought that it was something to be desired to make her wise: and she took it. I believe one reason why she took it lay in the attraction of the forbidden. This is part of the problem of human nature, and part of the explanation of a great deal of the moral morass we are in in our day. Men and women are going after that which is forbidden. The more they look at it, the more they are aware that it is forbidden; the more they sense the forbiddenness, the more they want it. They covet it, and the coveting becomes a craving that sooner, rather than later, overcomes them completely. There is an inclination towards the forbidden.

We must emphasise, of course, that temptation is not sin. Be quite clear about that. Temptation is not sin. Martin Luther said, "You cannot stop the crows flying over your head, but you can stop them building their nests in your hair." That is a vivid way of expressing the point. To be aware of temptation is not sin. But when we allow the look, the thought and the coveting to develop, then desire grows to craving and we want it, no matter the consequences. But God says, "You shall not covet." We must be as practical as possible, and to do so we need to learn the avenues along which we are most likely to be tempted. Then, at the gateway to these avenues, with the help of this commandment, we must learn to watch and pray.

Turn to Luke 12:13-21. At a time when matters of tremendous importance were being spoken about by the Son of God, there was one man in the congregation whose mind was completely fixed on possessions. It seems that his father had died and that his brother was being somewhat dilatory in getting the estate organised, registered and divided amongst the family. The man interrupted the sermon with a plea to Jesus to urge the brother to divide the inheritance. What an exposure of where his interest lay! Jesus said to all of them, using this man's request as an illustration:

"Take heed, and beware of all covetousness; for a man's life does not consist in the abundance of his possessions."

But it is covetousness with regard to possessions that can so easily and so permanently anchor the soul to the world.

Turn to another section of Scripture, the wise words of Proverbs 30:7- 9:

> "Two things I ask of thee; deny them not to me before I die: Remove far from me falsehood and lying; give me neither poverty nor riches; feed me with the food that is needful for me, lest I be full and deny thee, and say, 'Who is the Lord?' or lest I be poor, and steal, and profane the name of my God."

We should mark these verses in our Bibles and remember where to find them. They are wonderfully healthy and balanced. Do you see what they are saying? Let God have the ordering of our lives, to give or to withhold; to decide on the proportion of the giving or the withholding; not too much and not too little of wealth, pleasure, success and trials, and so to keep a right, healthy and manageable balance in our lives.

There are some people, even Christians, who put themselves under pressure and intolerable strain both by wrong self-indulgence and by wrong self-denial, the kind of strain which, if it does not break them, certainly limits their usefulness. They are trying to run their own lives. Even over-busyness can stem from coveting. We want to be in on everything. We want to let other people *see* that we are in on everything. Sometimes, for reasons that belong to our own complicated personalities, we are trying to prove to ourselves that we are of real value. We must learn to see that our lives are being dominated by a spirit of coveting, which spirit is forbidden. Turn to Hebrews 13:5:

> "Keep your life free from love of money, and be content with what you have; for he has said, 'I will never fail you nor forsake you.' "

We need to amplify the word "money". It is wider than just cash. It involves all sorts of things that come into the category of possessions, and the desire to be rich may have more to do with position and popularity than with money. Note also that it is not money itself, but love of money that is the problem, and it is not necessarily a lot of money that is involved. Keep yourself free from the love of money and be content with what you have. It takes deliberate effort. Turn to 1 Timothy 6:6-10:

> "There is great gain in godliness with contentment; for we brought nothing into the world, and we cannot take anything out of the world; but if we have food and clothing, with these we shall be content. But those who desire to be rich fall into temptation, into a snare, into many senseless and hurtful desires that plunge men into ruin

and destruction. For the love of money is the root of all evils; it is through this craving that some have wandered away from the faith and pierced their hearts with many pangs."

Godliness and contentment go together. These last two references in Hebrews and Timothy put great emphasis on the goodness and faithfulness of God. This is important. Many things cause us to go back to the doctrine of God. Do we think of Him as being cruel, as if His main objective was to deny us the things that we long for, in order to hurt us? Can that possibly be the God who spared not even His own Son, but delivered Him up to death on the Cross for us and for our salvation? Of course God is not hard! His whole heart of love is set upon us to bless us. We may well say at times, "I don't know how this denial in my life can be a blessing! I find it very difficult to cope with." I would certainly give you my sympathy if you feel that way. I do not profess to understand all God's ways. But we must take the attitude of faith and be prepared to trust the God of our salvation. Take as a last Scripture reference Philippians 4:11,12:

"Not that I complain of want; for I have learned, in whatever state I am, to be content. I know how to be abased (knocked down), and I know how to abound (be lifted up); in any and all circumstances I have learned the secret of facing plenty and hunger, abundance and want."

Paul is honest enough to admit he had *learned* this attitude of faith and contentment. There is no suggestion that it came easily, and indeed the learning may have taken a long time. If Paul stayed with friends who had very little he would be grateful to them, and to God, for sharing their "crust of bread". If he stayed with those who had plenty (and some ministered to Paul with great generosity) he would likewise be grateful to them and to God.

It needs God's grace to cope rightly with abundance, because when we are given a lot materially or spiritually it is all too easy to take it for granted, to forget God, to become selfish, even discontented, wanting more. That is how we end up coveting, and even become critical of God. It is vital for us to learn to be grateful and content with God's ordering of our lives; if we refuse to learn this we miss so much, particularly as He may still lead us to work and serve in a place where there is very little of all the "blessing" we take so much for granted.

Contentment, in all circumstances, has to be learned. When we begin to learn to be content we discover there is no need to covet, and we begin to be able to rejoice and to be really glad when someone is blessed with what we do not have.

Let me ask a question. Why are so many Christians discontented? It begins when our eyes and hearts are centred upon self rather than on Christ. Paul described coveting in his letter to the Ephesians as idolatry and that is what it is (Ephesians 5:5). Coveting is putting our will and our desires before God. Coveting has to do with the great tyrant self: "I want." But self has to die.

We are left with the alternatives of coveting or contentment. Do we not believe that all our life is planned for us? There is a hymn that sums it up well:

> I would not have the restless will
>   That hurries to and fro,
> Seeking for some great thing to do,
>   Or secret thing to know;
> I would be treated as a child
>   And guided where I go.
>
> So I ask Thee for the daily strength
>   To none that ask denied,
> And a mind to blend with outward life
>   While keeping at Thy side;
> Content to fill a little space,
>   If Thou be glorified. (Waring)

You shall not covet. The God who loves us dearly says, "Trust Me." This is peace and love and joy and hope. Are we not deeply moved when we think of the Almighty God, looking at us and saying so personally, "Trust Me"? Is there any reason why we should not? No! Are there any reasons why we should? Yes! Look back over the years and trace His goodness and mercy that have followed us. Now look to the future and listen to Paul's great affirmation:

"My God will supply every need of yours according to his riches in glory in Christ Jesus" (Philippians 4:19).

You shall not covet. There is absolutely no need to.

CONCLUSION

"And he said to him, "You shall love the Lord your God with all your heart, and with all your soul, and with all your mind. This is the great and first commandment. And the second is like it, You shall love your neighbour as yourself" (Matthew 22:37-39).

"If we say we have no sin, we deceive ourselves, and the truth is not in us. If we confess our sins, he is faithful and just, and will forgive our sins and cleanse us from all unrighteousness. If we say we have not sinned, we make him a liar, and his word is not in us.

My little children, I am writing this to you so that you may not sin; but if any one does sin, we have an advocate with the Father, Jesus Christ the righteous; and he is the expiation for our sins, and not for ours only but also for the sins of the whole world.

And by this we may be sure that we know him, if we keep his commandments" (1 John 1:8-2:3).

"If you love me, you will keep my commandments" (John 14:15).